WACO-

ADVANCE PRAISE FOR *THE PRIVATE LIVES OF PUBLIC BIRDS*

"I'm a serious backyard birder with a library of over a hundred bird books. Gedney's is now one of my top favorites. His lyrical and deeply felt insights, in particular about bird language, enable us to see that common birds are anything but."

—**AMY TAN**, author of *The Joy Luck Club*

"*The Private Lives of Public Birds* is an affectionate love song to our most familiar feathered neighbors. Grounded in science but watered by the heart of a poet, this intimate and personal look at the lives of the birds we see every day invites us to slow down and look again."

—**JOHN MUIR LAWS**, author of *The Laws Guide to Drawing Birds*

"Gedney has opened wide a portal for any and all, novice or expert, to enter a world of immediate avian wonder. With the help of ornithologists and poets and authors from the past—be they William Leon Dawson, Henry David Thoreau, or creation stories of the Western Mono—Gedney gathers together nuggets of goldfinch and treasures in feathers to be enjoyed whether we are gazing out our office window, stuck in traffic, or actively seeking."

—**KEITH HANSEN**, author of *Hansen's Field Guide to the Birds of the Sierra Nevada*

"Jack Gedney's book mingles science, story, and poetry, inviting readers to become immersed in the world of close-to-home birdlife—not to just look at birds, but to look *again* with attention, stillness, study, and curiosity. This book awakens all of our senses, making every step outside the door an opportunity for joy and belonging."

—**LYANDA LYNN HAUPT**, author of *Rooted* and *Mozart's Starling*

"What fun to follow Jack's curiosity as he bikes and birds and reads, bringing together dozens of human voices to deepen his essays, from Miwok and Yokuts stories, to a range of writers such as Li Bai, Kurt Vonnegut, Mary Austin, Bernd Heinrich, and even Joanna Newsom."

—**ALLEN FISH**, director of the Golden Gate Raptor Observatory, Golden Gate National Parks Conservancy

"I can't remember the last time I started smiling during a preface, couldn't put the book down, continued smiling through chapter one (on the brown scratcher), two (the blue squawker), and beyond. What a delight! This book is filled with such wonderful perspectives on the supposedly ordinary birds all around us."

—**DONALD KROODSMA**, author of *The Singing Life of Birds*

THE PRIVATE LIVES OF PUBLIC BIRDS

LEARNING TO LISTEN TO THE BIRDS WHERE WE LIVE

JACK GEDNEY

ILLUSTRATIONS BY ANNA KUŚ PARK

Heyday, Berkeley, California

"Vulture," copyright © 1963 by Garth Jeffers and Donnan Jeffers; from THE SELECTED POETRY OF ROBINSON JEFFERS by Robinson Jeffers. Used by permission of Random House, an imprint and division of Penguin Random House LLC. All rights reserved.
"Oda al picaflor," NUEVAS ODAS ELEMENTALES © Pablo Neruda, 1956, and Fundación Pablo Neruda.

Library of Congress Cataloging-in-Publication Data

Names: Gedney, Jack, 1989- author.
Title: The private lives of public birds : learning to listen to the birds where we live / Jack Gedney.
Description: Berkeley, California : Heyday, [2022] | Includes bibliographical references.
Identifiers: LCCN 2021046932 (print) | LCCN 2021046933 (ebook) | ISBN 9781597145749 (paperback) | ISBN 9781597145756 (epub)
Subjects: LCSH: Birds--California--Identification.
Classification: LCC QL684.C2 G43 2022 (print) | LCC QL684.C2 (ebook) | DDC 598.09794--dc23/eng/20211020
LC record available at https://lccn.loc.gov/2021046932
LC ebook record available at https://lccn.loc.gov/2021046933

Cover Art: Anna Kuś Park
Cover Design: Ashley Ingram
Interior Design/Typesetting: Ashley Ingram

Published by Heyday
P.O. Box 9145, Berkeley, California 94709
(510) 549-3564
heydaybooks.com

Printed in East Peoria, Illinois, by Versa Press, Inc.

10 9 8 7 6 5 4 3 2 1

FSC
www.fsc.org
MIX
Paper from
responsible sources
FSC® C005010

For Lena

CONTENTS

PREFACE

This is a book about fifteen familiar neighborhood birds of California. None are rare, all are found in a large portion of the state, and each of them brightens up my trip to work in a midsize town of Northern California.

This is also a book about different ways of seeing, hearing, and thinking about the natural world that will allow any encounter with a bird to add richness to your life. I often discuss ecology and evolution, because these are helpful tools for making sense of what the birds are up to and why they are the way they are. The objectivity of science helps prevent erroneous interpretation. I also often invite poets or opinionated old naturalists to share their points of view, because subjectivity is an invaluable ingredient in enthusiasm. My agenda is for greater daily human happiness through birds, and I've personally found the ideal prescription for this to be a good strong dose of both knowledge and instinctive delight.

Aldo Leopold found it enlightening to reflect on his "plant biases." This gave him an invigorating awareness of the fact that while he loved all trees, he was in love with pines. Lin Yutang gives a similar weight to the subjective in his definition of education as the development of good taste, rather than the accumulation of measurable knowledge. I hope this book will help you develop a taste for birds, and a taste *in* birds—to find the birds you are in love with.

CHAPTER 1
THE BROWN BIRD

California Towhee, *Melozone crissalis*

What bird means California to me?

We have specialties such as condors, California thrashers, and yellow-billed magpies, but for most of us such birds are not part of our daily lives, and nor are they for me. There are others more familiar, but which have less particularly Californian flavor —mourning doves or robins, for instance. Among our most intimate of neighbors, there is also a smaller set of brilliant birds that are more distinctive to our state, such as the lovely little lyrist miscalled the lesser goldfinch or the always scheming scrub-jay, planter of the oaks. These are birds I endlessly admire, and would regret to leave behind.

But I don't choose my closest friends for their musical inventiveness, or measure my sympathies by a scale of intelligence and industry. You can be plain and unmusical, with no claims to genius, and yet receive my unstinted affection. There are some people who simply stand for home, who are inseparably intermingled with a place and with ourselves. There is a bird like this for me: the brown bird, or California towhee, a friend who never fades away.

Outside of the mountains, almost every yard and city park in the state has its resident pair, two clay-colored, clumsy figures poking around the path as they search for fallen seeds. You've surely seen them: oversized and long-tailed sparrows, almost uniformly plain in their earthy suits save for a spot of rust beneath their tails. Towhees hardly hide, but hop around in imperturbable placidity, sedate and unalarmed. They are weak flyers who don't migrate, but stay put throughout the year. A few are found in Oregon, but the overwhelming majority of California towhees indeed belong to California, when you count both the upper and the lower. For millions of Californians, this is the bird of home.

Imagine waking up one morning, on one of those days when the world doesn't quite cohere, when your surroundings for whatever reason feel alien and unfamiliar. But then you hear birds outside the window, a steady call-and-answer chirping, and you no longer feel so lost. It tells you that all is well, no threats are near, and that the pair is still together in their inevitable attachment. This is the voice that says: you are not a stranger here, and you are where you belong.

This book will help you find that reassurance and bedrock at-home feeling. It will help you learn those sights and sounds, so that each day the birds will share their meanings. A landscape that was empty will fill with familiar old companions, and mornings that were silent will sing with a hundred perfect voices.

If you have passed your years without that sense of home among the birds of California, then today can be the day toward which your life was ripening. Today can be the morning when your eyes and ears spring open. You will learn how to see colors. We'll start—right now—with brown.

Every True Name Has Its Music

Let us keep the most beautiful and fitting among common names, and work for their general adoption. . . . History and romance, music and hard common sense are in them.

—Julia Ellen Rogers, *Trees Worth Knowing*, 1917

If you wish to know the birds and make them companions in your life, learning their names is indispensable. In some cases, these might not be the names in the official registers. We often set aside the strict designations of our birth certificates in favor of alternatives that feel more personal and deeply accurate. If anything, we should do this more often with birds, whose official appellations are determined by precedent and committee, rather than bestowed by thoughtful, loving parents and then made permanent by years of self-identification.

This particular bird is a good example of the pitfalls of our formal systems. The American Ornithological Society has dubbed the species the California towhee, deriving that odd word from the call of an entirely different bird, the eastern towhee. Our bird makes no such sound. Her scientific name is *Melozone crissalis*. *Melozone* means "banded cheek," in reference to a Central American relative. Our bird has no banded cheek. The specific epithet *crissalis* is an awkward bit of faux Latin meaning "of the crissum," or more colloquially "the one with the rump." At least this name is acknowledging a trait that belongs to the California bird: her one slight distinction of plumage is that rusty red patch underneath her tail. But "of the crissum" is ineloquent to everyone, except perhaps to certain wry classicists, who might find it amusing—*crissum* is not a real Latin noun for "undertail coverts" but a modern derivative from a verb of ancient earthiness that has inspired centuries' worth of sheepish euphemism among both ornithologists and translators of Roman literature. (My favorites include "a certain action of the parts" and "blandishing waggle-bottom" for one who performs the action.)

No one who actually lives with these birds would independently decide to call them "band-cheeks." No Native Californian would ever have thought to name them "towhees." I wouldn't object to dubbing them "rusty waggle-bottoms," but I think I stand alone. So what can we do today? One option I enjoy is to draw on the rich reserves of folk and traditional names. In Spanish, they've long been known as *rascadores*, or scratchers, which I find both apt and catchy. The early settlers of the West called them names like drab or brown chippie, which concisely and without pretension summarize their dominant impressions of appearance and of sound (*chip!*). Simplest of all and at the very bottom rung of all possible humility is "brown bird," which has the recommendation of Joanna Newsom, California's minstrel of the magical mundane:

> Last week, our picture window
> produced a half word,
> heavy and hollow,
> hit by a brown bird
>
> . . .
>
> Then in my hot hand, she slumped her sick weight.
> We tramped through the poison oak, heartbroke and inchoate.

These verses demonstrate a simple truth: some names are consistent with poetry and feeling and some aren't. Try to insert "California towhee" into those lyrics. To force your life into taxonomy's terms is to rob it of warmth.

These several names are not mutually exclusive. I rotate nicknames for my friends, depending on which aspect of their character is at that moment resonating in my affections. But I always seek to use those names that pass Rogers's test: seek out what is "most beautiful and fitting," the names of history and common sense. Choose the names with music in them. Find the names with which you can address each bird, not just with knowledge, but with intimacy—names worthy of your friends.

The Familiar Grows Dear

The definitive statement on the brown bird was published in 1923 by William Leon Dawson, in his magisterially idiosyncratic and humane *Birds of California*:

> Familiar objects, whatever their worth, come to be dear to us through association. There is, honestly, no particular reason why we should be fond of this prosy creature, save that he is always around. In appearance, the bird is a bit awkward, slovenly, and uncouth; or at least, we are obliged to see him oftenest in every-day duds, and he seems to have no company manners. And for color—never was a more hopeless drab. . . . Yet I suppose there are few Californians who would willingly spare the homely, matter-of-fact presence of this bird under foot. Brown towhees are just birds—the same way most of us are just folks.

We will hear again from Dawson, in part for his encyclopedic knowledge of the birds of my state, but above all for his unmatched capacity for turning knowledge into appreciation. Here he takes certain seldom-praised traits of the brown bird—ubiquity, awkwardness, and plainness—and finds their sum to be a character no one would wish to lose. I can corroborate his generalization: every-day Californians constantly engage me in conversations about birds, and no bird provokes more unsolicited glee and superficially inexplicable delight.

But the secret of this puzzle is not hard to unlock, once you look a little closer. Ubiquity and plainness are not conventionally exciting qualities, but it doesn't at all follow that they are grounds for disdain or dislike. What they are grounds for is familiarity.

You'll find the California scratcher in most of inhabited California: in yards and parks and weedy fields, as well as in woodland and chaparral. They thrive in our towns and suburbs and avoid only the dense forests and high mountains. They love the edges of roadways and find humans fitting neighbors.

Within our yards themselves, they are unusually unhesitant among the cautious mass of birds: chippies are famous for their tendency to hop through open doorways, seeking seeds buried in the carpet, and for attacking their own reflections in windows during the height of the nesting season's fervor. They don't understand those doors and windows well, I have to admit. But few birds assert with such confidence that our homes fall within their domain. This can get them into trouble, as in those unwinnable battles with mirrors. We see brown birds in their frequent foolish moments. But if you've never seen a person's failings, it means you don't yet fully know them. Brown birds are the rare birds whose blunders take place where we can see them.

"He is always around," says Dawson, to sum up this simple ubiquity. "There were brown chippies in the door-yard, brown chippies around the barns, and brown chippies in the brush till one got tired of the sight of them," writes Florence Merriam Bailey to state the same fact and her initial sharing of the general disdain. But she ultimately finds herself in a similar state of somewhat bemused affection, ruefully conceding that she had been led astray by the common temptation "to undervalue what is at hand and overvalue the rare or distant."

When it comes to the next trait Dawson mentions—the brown bird's superlatively uncouth and slovenly comportment—the unfiltered world of old bird books continues to pull few punches. "The bird is a rustic with the stolidity of the peasant," writes Ralph Hoffman in the 1927 classic *Birds of the Pacific States*. Most birds give a more neutral impression of personality and fail to provoke such opinionated commentaries. Even detractors can't help but be engaged by brown birds. And so I read Hoffman's denigration with delight, gleeful that this favorite of mine has made an impression that clearly overpowered the feeble resistance of intellectualized good taste.

My standard riposte when I hear others engaging in profuse praise of some exotic beauty of a bird is "Eh, it's no brown chippie," which I think the pantheon of American ornithologists would have to concede is a quite inarguable point.

There are, of course, biological correlations to their plainness. The most obvious evolutionary force that determines color is camouflage value. Brown birds like it brown: dust, dirt, and our characteristically droughty summers are their native element. Within it, they are singularly well colored and therefore comfortable feeding out in the open, hopping about in our cleared paths and unforested yards. They are so familiar to us in part because they are so unfurtive in their daily lives: plain colors reduce the frequency of panic and the constant urge to hide.

We can see brown birds every day, feeding calmly in the open. We *hear* them even more. As a general habit, chippies forage together in their permanent pairs, maintaining contact with continuous metallic *chip!* notes, reminiscent of a pair of smoke alarms with dying batteries. Few would cite this as the most intrinsically melodious of bird sounds, but it is perhaps the most mundane: there are few other birds whose daily discourse is so present in our lives.

Brown birds surround our houses, blend in comfortably with our gardens, and carry on their conversations outside our windows. Their case makes plain an easily overlooked but actually quite obvious fact: that our real affections don't rely on the commonly cited reasons for birdwatching excitement, such as rarity, brightness of color, or beauty of song. What they rely on is familiarity, with which no bird is more overflowing.

If you wish to know the birds, don't become obsessed with penetrating the distance and timidity of the shy, elusive beauties. Embrace instead the nearness and self-possession of those who feel at home when by your side.

The Nation of Two

There is, I think, a second reason why we feel so drawn toward this bird. With just a little attention, we soon see that our dull and dusty neighbor is neither a random passing individual nor an indistinguishable member of a flock, but a precise half of a single little family: there are exactly two brown birds in your yard. All year round they stay together and defend their territory in partnership, two scratchers side by side.

Most of the observations I've described testify to this central fact about the brown birds' social lives. That sense of steady presence reveals that they do not move: those are the same scratchers that you see in June and in December. The male's shadowboxing at the window reveals his firm antagonism toward intruders: there is only one other chipping bird whose company he accepts. And even their plain plumage suggests the nature of their love lives, which are steadiness incarnate.

The typical countervailing force that leads many birds away from discreet and sensible colors is the need to attract a mate. Male birds are often brighter because females more often do the choosing, using vibrant colors as an indicator of genetic sound-ness, nutritional condition, and the general competence needed to secure sufficient food and stay alive despite carrying around that blaring billboard to predators.

You consequently see those bright males more in species whose bonds are short lived and ephemeral, where females need to make a quick evaluation with each spring that rolls around. Brown birds are less subject to this imperative because they don't remate each year. Instead they pair up once and never part. You can see this correlation of plainness and long-term monogamy in numerous birds, from black ravens to gray titmice. Birds that stick together have less need for dangerous bright colors.

Not just their plumage but their plain voices echo this same story. In addition to their keep-in-touch notes, male brown birds also have a springtime song. It's easy to recognize, essentially repeating a number of those sharp chirps in an accelerating, "bouncing ball" pattern that starts with a few bold *chips!* before quickly petering out.

Spring birdsong is one of the glories of existence. I'll go out to the woods, I'll go out to the fields, and I'll go out to the cor-ner park to hear the numerous ecstatic ensembles of the sea-son. Purple finches rolling upward in great revolving crescendos! Fencepost-topping meadowlarks bugling to the sky as far as I can see! And then among the mighty trumpets and the sweeping woodwinds and the woodpeckers' percussion I hear a hesitant, soft tinkling, like a cheap, mistuned triangle that is struck a few times and then hur-riedly set down with an embarrassed clatter. That's the chippie!

Dawson also found ironically hyperbolic enthusiasm the most rewarding lens through which to listen to the brown bird's spring performance:

> This overworked note must do duty for song. For this pur-pose it is furbished up a bit, brightened, intensified, and

aspirated, till it sounds like a sibilant squeak. The singer mounts a bush or tree-top, or the comb of a roof, and with uttermost ardor delivers himself of such sentiments as these, *tsick tsick tsick tsick tsick*. Listen! O ye Muses, and pause, Satyrs, in your mad gambols. Orpheus will smite the lyre again: *Tsick tsick tsick tsick tsick*.

To note the comparative simplicity of the towhee song is not merely an expression of irrelevant human preference but a recognition of the different evolutionary functions that song fulfills for different species. For musical mockingbirds and the like, long and variable songs are crucial ways of demonstrating male fitness: females prefer the most elaborate performances. But in other birds, the predominant purpose of song is territorial declaration or simple indication of unmated status. That seems to be the case here, with the drab bachelors abruptly ceasing almost all song upon the appearance of a female and with songs highly uniform and consistent, rather than plastic and complex for more meaningful comparison.

Visually and vocally, the story is the same. Brown birds omit compromising surface displays from their evolutionary strategy because they have opted for a very different plan: find someone and never leave her. Scratchers mate for life, they stay together all year round, and divorce is nearly unknown. This already puts them in the minority of songbirds, most of which are monogamous only within each nesting season.

The clinching piece of the brown birds' romantic credentials is their passion for "duets," synchronized bouts of rapid squeaking with their mate. Many male birds sing, but only some 7 percent engage in these reciprocal performances. Chippies do this throughout the year, peaking during nesting, when they've been recorded duetting an average of seven times per hour. The basic pattern goes like this: when several feet or yards apart, whether in sight or just beyond, one bird will begin its duet-squeaking, and the other will immediately respond. The two then rush together in a jubilant cascade of synchronizing squeals and end up side by side in gratified reassurance. There are some variations in context, but the net effect is partner coordination and continuous reinforcement of the pair bond.

In his novel *Mother Night*, Kurt Vonnegut describes the insular and self-sufficient connection between the hero and his wife, who contentedly declare themselves an independent Nation of Two. The brown birds far exceed us in realizing that vision, rejecting all intruders for the full measure of their lives, save for the few months of rearing children who soon must leave their parents. Scratchers stick together. There is nothing more fundamental to their character.

So when you meet that chipping brown bird, seek her partner close at hand. Transform those piercing calls from mere noises into words, for there is no clearer conversation than that constant affirmation. Bright and surface finery is the suit of ephemeral emotions, but this simple coat of clay is molded by a bond that does not alter. It is not merely feather deep, but lasts through every molt and season.

CHAPTER 2
THE GARDEN'S KEEPER

California Scrub-Jay, *Aphelocoma californica*

Amid the greens and browns of California, there is one blue figure encountered far more often than any other. You may find bluebirds in the open fields, and even lovely buntings scattered here and there. But the scrub-jay stalks the parks and suburbs, enters both the dusty chaparral and the dim woods along the creek, and above all tends the oaks in every place they grow.

I love to hear them raucously appear, mounting to a treetop or claiming space at the feeding station. Boldly blue and white beneath, there is no one for whom you could mistake them. No other backyard bird is so bristling with determination and intent. All birds seem alert, but for most this awareness seems primarily a readiness to flee. That is not the jay's case. Her alertness feels like the precursor to some bold action that will not be turned aside. She squawks, lands, looks around, weighs threats and opportunities. She takes a few of the nuts I leave out for her and flies off to add them to her scattered, hidden stores.

These jays are the keepers of the California woods. Now they also guard our towns and neighborhoods, and shape the landscapes that we live in. The forests hold the crested Steller's jays, but the scrub-jays permeate the far greater portion of our state. These uncrowned birds (*Aphelocoma* means "smooth-haired") are the less glamorous and less admired cousins, often misunderstood, or accused of harshness and cruelty. I hope to exonerate them from those charges. But this bird deserves more than exoneration: she is the genius of our native creatures.

There are many clever corvids, and this most Californian ranks high among them, using tools, recording time, and interpreting the intentions of other birds and people. Most striking of her many talents is her memory for places: she knows our homes better than we or any others do. What purpose does she labor for with all her memory and craft? She works to plant the oaks and keep the acorns safe from harm. Today we live beneath those canopies, California's endless temples built by centuries of jays.

She acts as if she owns the trees, and if anyone can stake the claim, it's she: her mothers and fathers planted those seeds long ago, and she carries on their work. If you are ever tempted to dismiss the California jays, or mislabel them as destroyers, then step out into the forest beneath those thousand spreading trees and ask yourself this question:

What seeds have I sown?

Let Me Hear Those Crashing Cymbals

My pledges

Sung in a voice

Like that of the jay;

Even when I cry

You do not lend an ear.

—Ōya No Urazumi

I am an enthusiastic advocate for opening windows. You get to hear so much more, from the high, thin whistles of waxwings in the winter trees to the liquid, snipping chatter of summer swallows overhead. When I open my windows, I can hear almost as many birds as if I were outside. When I close them, I mostly just hear jays. Other birds are muted and submerged, but the jays pass through the glass as if it were paper, and cannot be excluded.

Jays' calls give them their name, an onomatopoeic rendering of their loud and grating monosyllables. The name was first applied in England to the wide-ranging Eurasian jay—the same bird Urazumi knew in Japan—but is quite appropriate to the related birds of North America, whether the blue jay of the East or our own California scrub-jay. I grab a fistful of bird books from my shelf and discover a uniformity unusual in the subjective field of listening: "harsh and angry-sounding" says Sibley; "harsh, metallic," says Pieplow; "very harsh" says Hoffman; and "loud, harsh, scolding," says Pete Dunne. They are in perfect agreement about our bird's exceptional, window-piercing quality.

It isn't *wrong* to call it harsh; the agreement of these authors reflects a normal human reaction, and the term is a perfectly useful shorthand for practical identification. But if you stop at the application of that label, then you run the risk of Urazumi's uncharitable beloved, of disdaining the speaker whose voice you find unlovely. Lend an ear to the squawkers. They pledge their faith, cry for compassion, and always speak with meaning.

This is more true of birds in general than people tend to acknowledge, and even more true in the case of jays. What you hear are not mere sounds, but words, drawn from a vocabulary we are far from fully deciphering. Jays have calls for preemptive display flights in their territory and calls for active aggression should intruders arrive, warnings of predators that distinguish both identity and location, and numerous phrases of intimate and undiscovered meaning given only in private conversation with their mate.

I find this last phenomenon of "quiet song" extremely intriguing. We're just beginning to realize how many birds perform these quiet "songs"—complex communications shared between mated birds—because they're so much harder to hear and record than the classic loud songs of courtship or territorial display. Jays don't perform loud songs, but both males and females engage in quiet song. To hear a jay speak softly can revise your whole understanding of their character, as when you first see any blustering tough guy in a moment of sentimental domesticity.

This is not to say that their "tough" moments of loud squawking are without their utility and value. After all, those calls are often warnings, advertisements of danger that protect their families and neighboring birds of all species. A superficial listener might hear that loudest clamor, triggered by some hawk or cat, and notice only the sound of violence and aggression. But these are actually the moments when jays set aside their personal squabbles, when they lay down their territorial insistence to unite with previously bickering neighbors against a greater danger. This is a fundamental thing to remember about the loudest warnings of the jays: they are not partisan but universal, and all the birds that could be victims receive the benefits of those calls.

But even with no exculpatory knowledge, even considering this voice as an abstract bundle of tones and timbres, I would not willingly lose this sound from my life. One of our jay's traditional names is "blue squawker," and I embrace the term. (*Scrub-jay* is another eastern-originating title of misleading imprecision: ornithologists named the more scrub-limited Florida version first and then applied the title more broadly, but our bird extends beyond pure scrublands.) Squawking is simply what they do. And far from being an unalleviated disruption to the serenity of my life, that squawking adds texture, contrast, and spice to what would otherwise be a more boring world.

The Preston Sturges comedy *Unfaithfully Yours* tells the story of a brilliant conductor. In rehearsal, he admonishes his percussionist for an inadequately crashing performance on the cymbals. The musician mildly explains that he was raised to never be too loud or vulgar. His leader corrects him, overriding such petty concerns as politeness and decorum: "Be vulgar by all means, but let me hear that brazen laugh!"

The woods need jays as orchestras need cymbals. When I hear that defiant, vulgar warning break like crashing copper through the chatter of the less alert, I smile with relish as I recite the exhortation under my breath: "Let me hear that brazen laugh!"

My second principle of knowing birds: after names, what you must turn your attention to are voices. Recognizing words—the meaning of a given call—is good, but words are clumsy things, like written notes of music. The real music is not on the page. It takes a voice to clothe our skeleton language in melody and timbre, and make it come to life.

The Opposite of a Bully

The most frequent accusation leveled against jays is of violence, both predatory and temperamental. Jays do eat small birds, especially their eggs and nestlings. But when people hear harsh voices, they seem to think jays invariably angry, and when they see a jay displace the finches at a feeder, they think them habitually aggressive. The connection between these common observations and a life of constant killing is tenuous. I think they are condemned mostly on the basis of unfriendly character witnesses.

How many helpless infant juncos do squawkers really consume? Jays are flexible omnivores, but their favorite food is clearly acorns, and even in spring's profusion of baby birds, their mainstays are caterpillars and grasshoppers. Back in the days of science by mass dissection, one researcher opened up the stomachs of 326 scrub-jays and found remnants of other birds in a grand total of eight of them. Native Californians were more attuned to jays' real food hanging heavy in the oaks, and so came closer to the truth: "I do not believe that you can hit me [with your arrows]. I eat nothing but acorns. That is what makes me so lively," Jay explains in one Miwok story. And who are we to talk? In comparison with humans, jays' impacts on bird populations are clearly far smaller and more ecologically bounded.

A good portion of backyard jay critics never actually observe those nestling depredations that do occur. What they see is the displacement of small birds at their feeders when the larger jays arrive to a soundtrack rich in squawking. I've dabbled in every genre of bird feeding and found a dozen ways of mitigating conflict more effective than waving an angry fist in the jays' direction. Sometimes, I like to lay down a trail of millet for the brown birds, doves, and sparrows, or hang a tube of thistle seeds for the goldfinches and siskins—the squawkers don't care for either food. Many friends of mine put cages around their sunflower feeders to allow access only to the harmlessly petite. Small but feisty hummingbirds sip their sugar water without much opposition—until *they* go looking for a fight.

So consider this the next time you hear a jay, his strident summons ringing out. The small birds step aside, but they often are not the subject of his shouting. He may be speaking to his rivals, as nearly all birds do, to keep them from his nest and territory. Or he may be warning of a larger threat, an alarm that benefits all his smaller neighbors. This is the opposite of bullying—not preying on the weaker but holding firm against all threats, regardless of their size.

Who stands up against the hawk and cat? Not the goldfinch or the dove. The blue squawker swoops close and cries, until no one can ignore him. Rival jays and sometime victims both lay aside past squabbles when they hear that call, for they know that they can trust it. We're the only ones who still mistake it for a bully's threat or a merely noisy nuisance.

So let the cymbals crash and the brazen laughter sound. One day we will learn to hear in them the warner of the woods.

The California Genius

The corvid family, which includes the jays, crows, and ravens, are generally considered the most complex thinkers of our continent's birdlife. Sophisticated language and social structures; strong memories for places, individuals, and facts; the use of tools and multi-step problem solving—all of these point to cognitive abilities that we collectively label as intelligence. California's scrub-jays deserve this recognition on a dozen such counts.

They use rudimentary tools by identifying optimal "anvil" sites to which they will bring their acorns for securely held cracking. (Track a squawker to his forked-branch anvil and investigate it afterward—you will find the wood worn smooth like the fir slab to which the bottle opener was mounted at the trail crew camp where I spent a summer. Both receive the friction that comes with frequent loving use.) Jays have a complex vocal array that varies by speaker and addressee as well as situation. Their genus is generally known for its complex multigenerational social structures, although our California branch has reverted to Nations of Two for certain ecological reasons. And scrub-jays recognize individuals both of their own species and of humans, remembering their past behavior and predicting their future actions.

All of that is well worth keeping in mind. When you see jays and crows, recognize that they are engaging in something more like thinking as we know it than any other characters in this volume. Memory and reasoning are turning their gears. But there is one particular realm of cognition that stands out above all others in the scrub-jay's cabinet, and that is not some rudimentary form of human-like intelligence for which we condescendingly compliment them as aspirants to our level of cleverness, but something we flatly cannot do: they plant thousands of acorns and remember where they've put them.

Acorns ripen through the fall. To get through winter to spring's abundance of fresh insects, the squawkers rely on stored food, overwhelmingly those durable nuts. One study estimated their yearly caches at some 5,000–7,000 acorns for each bird, each individually buried an inch or so beneath the soil's surface. Perhaps half are recovered. Could you personally deposit 3,000 acorns in unmarked, hidden locations underground and then recover them months later? I couldn't.

Their other feats that tend to make the anthologies of avian cleverness are all offshoots of this caching behavior. They remember what they've stored and where, so that they can retrieve insects and other perishables first and save the long-lasting nuts for later. In experimental settings, they quickly learn what food will be reliably on offer and store the other, complementary items rather than more of the same. Most unique is their suspicion informed by personal experience: the jays who've practiced pilfering realize that observant bystanders could do the same, and make sure to recache their treasures out of sight.

But the talent that still amazes me as simply beyond our human power is that central skill at refinding thousands of objects, without maps or notes or signs. Jays study their few acres twelve months a year and memorize each inch of soil. They know the rocks and branches and the way the sun shines through them. Who is most at home on this patch of earth called California? The one who fills each corner with the food she needs to live, the blue guardian and gardener.

They Plant the Oaks

Now the eagle, who was the chief of all, sent off the victorious mountain people. He said: "You cannot live here any longer. You must go away. Where do you want to go?"

. . .

The bluejay said: "I am going to make trees grow over the hills."

—Yaudanchi Yokuts story

What does this look like?

In fall, the jays immerse themselves in the foliage of the oaks, wrestling off the acorns as they ripen. In summer it seemed as though they were always squawking and chasing everything in sight. Now they grow quiet: the nesting territoriality has relaxed, and food is so abundant that they no longer need to fight. They're also squawking less for a reason I can see: it seems as though every October squawker has an acorn in her mouth.

If they're not harvesting, they're planting. An acorn-laden jay hops along the ground, looking cautiously around. When she's satisfied that no one is watching, or at least no one who counts—the brown chippies, for example, are always ignored as insufficiently astute to merit consideration—she deposits the acorn on the soil, gives it a whack with her sturdy beak, verifies that the nail is being driven truly, then smacks again as needed to bury it beneath the surface.

Perhaps the most memorable moments are the slower ones that make you think, the puzzles of a tree's provenance that have no other explanation. I once lived in a suburb of ample yards, but only scattered remnant oaks from the days before the houses—

there wasn't a single oak tree within a hundred yards. So how did this sapling valley oak appear behind the tomatoes? And another over here against the fence? And what could make a blue oak sprout from within the potted rosemary?

A jay's recovery of three thousand acorns is an impressive feat. But it leaves three thousand more in the soil, largely safe from predators, at an ideal depth for germination, and distributed in numerous locations rather than concentrated in the unpromising shade of their parent tree. Acorns that simply fall on the surface very seldom grow up to be trees. Immediate consumption would destroy them, so they need someone who saves. Squirrels and rodents concentrate their stores and do not travel far.

How did oaks become the planet's most successful trees? By recruiting a winged blue genius to carefully plant their offspring, safe from danger, in places where they'll grow. You can overlay a global map of these two partners' ranges and see this story: oaks grow all around the world, but nowhere without jays. The oaks cannot do without their gardeners.

This doesn't mean that the oaks reward the jays with uninterrupted generosity. Like other masting trees, oaks don't produce a consistent amount of acorns each year. To do so would support a growing population of predators until there were few acorns left. Instead, they switch between years of modest production, years of overwhelming abundance, and years of utter scarcity. This is an effective strategy to combat the depredations of most predators of seeds and keep their numbers limited: strike them with intermittent years of famine. And all the jays' skills of storage do not exempt them from this fate.

Inevitably the acorns fail, perhaps one year out of five. In the wild lands where oaks are their main food source, many jays must leave when the acorns don't appear. They have to leave the home they've known, their lifelong partners scattered in the exodus. Jays are survivors: they will wander for the winter, find other oaks or other food. In spring they will return, hoping to reclaim their territory.

The California jays don't migrate and never willingly leave home. But if you live among the oaks and watch in the year the acorns fail, you may find that the woods grow quiet and miss their flash of blue. Famine and divorce may force a jay from the trees she's planted, stretching thin those ties to home. But the strongest ties are those that stretch and do not break. Her mind contains more memories than those of other birds, and in spring they fill her with a longing not for vague northward motion but for the place she knows. She flies, and flies, until out from that discontented winter she returns in refutation of defeat. She grasps the branch she's always grasped, and the world is whole again.

The Great Garden

Without the jays, the oak woodland as we know it could not exist. We criticize their occasional depredations upon the nests of smaller songbirds while ignoring their far more fundamental role as the chief architects of those birds' homes. How many oak titmice and acorn woodpeckers would there be if the jays did not plant the trees? When the acorn famine strikes, most of those other birds will stay, surviving in those planted trees while the gardeners learn exile. That fate can seem unfair.

Fortunately, the squawkers are resilient. They can travel, if they need to. They can store food more craftily than any other, but they can also find alternatives should their prudence not suffice. They are rooted to their woodland not by simple immobility but by a set of memories that outlives famine, exodus, and divorce and points them homeward in the spring. Flowers and insects are emerging, and they hear their garden calling.

The squawkers are the uncrowned jays, but I will let them no more go unsung. They have made these hills I love and covered them with trees. So when that brazen trumpet sounds, I salute the guardian and gardener, the ally of the oaks. I hear the warning of the watcher and know the woods still have their keeper. And when in some unattended corner where we've sown nothing but neglect, I find a new oak climbing skyward, then I share the triumph in their note. The crashing cymbals rise above our traffic, the undefeated instrument of the ever crescent orchestra of trees. Listen closer and you'll hear it in the echo of their voices: the forest past and future whispers in the leaves.

CHAPTER 3
I CAN HEAR WHEN THEY CALL

American Crow, *Corvus brachyrhynchos*

I have a simple formula for doubling the birds in your life: listen to the crows.

More Californians probably cross paths with them each day than with any other bird, although many fail to notice the meeting. Crows are the most ignored birds in America.

In some ways, they are a strange bird to overlook. The corvid family contains the most intelligent and socially complex birds of North America, which one might think would make them objects of interest and admiration. American crows are the great generalists of the family, with a continent-spanning range even wider than that of ravens, who, while not rare in California, are less enamored of human proximity—crows are the default corvid in urban and suburban settings. Where the two cousins in blackness overlap, recognize crows by their smaller size, more frequent occurrence in large flocks, and more flapping flight compared to the wide-winged soaring of the larger birds.

I see ravens some days. Every day I see crows. I see them from my window at home, and out in the parking lot at work. I see them at the corner playground and on the downtown streets. They perch in the trees, flap to the rooftops, walk on the pavement, and hop out of the way of approaching cars with one foot held in front of the other, imperturbably wrapped up in an insouciant lack of panic, as if they were performing some playful trotting that I've been too serious for since third-grade gym class.

Why look at crows? I am accompanied by black feathers, watched by black eyes, and discussed by black beaks everywhere I go. To ignore their constant conversation would be to enclose myself within a bubble every time I step outside, to be an always-indoor person, whether inside of doors or not.

I have only a mild interest in encouraging people to go out looking for birds. The more valuable revelation is that birds already surround you.

Crow Paradise Is Here and Now

The world was made by Prairie Falcon, Crow, and Coyote.
. . . These three are in the east now, watching the dam that they made, to see that it does not break and the impounded waters destroy the world.

—Creation story of the Western Mono

Crows have been here since before the beginning, according to the oldest stories of central California. When we now think of the changes the past centuries have brought to the natural world, we often focus on the idea that we live in fallen times: "the highway dust is over all," as Robert Frost's ovenbird laments. That's true for many birds, but not for this one. Modern human settlement displaced innumerable animals, but the transformation of North America also created "an Eden for crows." I see more of these birds today than the Mono did five hundred years ago.

At that time, California's crows were less abundant and more thinly distributed, without modern urban concentrations. Indigenous stories view them ecologically as scavengers, while centuries of European colonization considered them primarily as agricultural pests: crows were accused of stealing eggs, blinding newborn livestock, and above all feeding in great flocks on fields of corn and grains.

But where we go, they go. In the twentieth century, crows' concentration in agricultural areas was replaced by migration to urban areas, where human-provisioned food is even more reliable for the gleaners. Our broader changes to the landscape fit the preferences of crows: we create clearings in continuous forests, found irrigated oases in deserts, and plant lawns for foraging and trees for nesting in drained wetlands. These are the changes that create what John Marzluff and Tony Angell call an Eden for crows, adding up to "a nearly perfect arrangement of nesting and feeding habitat" and leading to an overall booming population. In the 1930s, a winter survey estimated a California-wide population of eighty-two thousand crows, spread among a number of rural roost sites. By the 1980s, all reported roosts were in urban locations, with a single roost in Yuba City estimated at one million crows. One million crows!

Now fewer crows shadow the poultry yards and cornfields than march among the parks and parking lots. Their movement to this new paradise has been encouraged by the increasing drawbacks of what at first seemed the unparalleled abundance of the farmlands, most notably shooting and disease. In the United States' more agricultural past, anticrow vitriol was more widely lethal. Governments and gun manufacturers sponsored crow hunts. Winter roosts were dynamited until the 1940s, killing tens of thousands of birds at a time. The result was not so much crow eradication as crow relocation: they moved to town, where both antipathy and trigger-readiness are much lower. People might complain about suburban crows—their noise or messiness or threat to smaller birds (which is easily overstated)—but this rarely reaches a point of deadly aggression.

The great threat to crows of late has been the advent of mosquito-transmitted West Nile virus, for which they are more at risk than any other bird in California. After the disease arrived here in the mid-2000s, one survey on mostly agricultural routes in the Sacramento Valley saw declines of 63 percent in crow counts from the 1990s, with the largest decreases in areas of mosquito-rich rice cultivation and lowest in areas of human habitation and associated vector control. The cities are safer.

As the world changed, so did they: crows persisted and thrived. From 1970 to 2019, California's winter crow population increased by over 400 percent. Sometimes we still fall into the error of thinking ourselves alone and separate, the unique possessors of these streets. But we've also built this place for crows, who prosper here among us. Today, a day without crows is a strange and empty silence and an aberration in my life.

Now I live within a double city, a town of people and a town of crows. To go out to the wild is to leave this bird behind, but here walkers chatter from the sidewalk, and the winged call from above. Running through all their varied conversation is a message I can hear:

Crow paradise is not a place unmarred by human hands. The age of crows was not the time before the plows and cars.

They Will Not Face the Night Alone

The sun settles behind the hill like a silent sinking stone. I see four crows in a line, steadily flapping toward the edge of town in the fading light. Orange glows from the horizon as it does from any dying fire, and the birds seem even blacker than they did during the day. At this distance, flesh and feathers dissolve into abstract forms, become holes cut through the planet's haze to show the night outside.

These receding black shapes are not the private plotting individuals that grab my attention in the day; now the crows show me only what they share in common. Another line follows, and another on a different tack, flying to converge somewhere out beyond my sight. Now I see the symbol clearer: these black-dashed lines across the sky are not mere lines but arrows, pointing to a single target. What they point toward is safety, and what they fly from is isolation, an enemy we share.

This is how crows live: they mate for life, and like many birds, the pair maintains a private territory in spring. Crow pairs are often joined by nonbreeding helpers, frequently offspring from the previous year, but also including older children or even unrelated adoptees. There may be a few of these helpers or there may be a dozen, and they help feed and protect the young, growing their own skills and experience before attempting to breed themselves.

In fall, when nesting is complete, most crows gather into larger roosting groups at night, which can contain hundreds or thousands of birds. Unlike most winter-flocking birds, they don't forget their partners and families: nonmigratory crows—as many are in California—continue to fly out to their territory as a group each day, foraging together until they return to the evening roost in those twilight arrows. The first benefit of the large group is safety: if you are ensconced within a thousand crows, you are unlikely to be seized by an owl in the night. Roosts also provide a chance to share information and meet others; adolescent or migratory birds can connect with local territory holders and join their foraging families.

This system allows crows the benefits of a Nation of Two— an established partner and a familiar territory—as well as the benefits of a larger flock: group safety, information about food sources, and opportunities to meet potential mates and allies. The essential requirement for such complexity is individual recognition, the ability to distinguish over long periods of time among a mate, a family member, a tolerated stranger, and a territorial rival. Such enduring fine-scale distinctions are muted in most flocking birds: the participants in a swirling mass of blackbirds or sandpipers treat all their peers roughly alike, with perhaps some in-the-moment deference to age or size.

With crows it's different. I see half a dozen crows walking around the soccer field looking for grubs when a family member returns from an errand. She drops from the sky and descends, gives a little series of short caws, and a few birds return her greeting without interruption to their foraging. But a few minutes later, an unwelcome neighbor attempts to simply fly by in silence and is greeted by a host of raucous voices, who rise into the air to escort him from the family territory. Crows have enemies and allies.

Another day: I see a bulky nest high in a pine, with one black head barely protruding. I assume it's the incubating or brooding female, and that the approaching bird carrying something in his beak is her mate. Then something subtle, and less common, occurs: another bird approaches and lands with a burden of his own—now there are *three* birds at the nest. Baby crows are the only birds in this book likely to have a big brother bring them food.

What does it mean to be part of a crow family? Members cooperate in defense and in feeding children—and in play. Crows compete at aerial acrobatics with their siblings, play tug-of-war with sticks, and like to belly-sled down snow-covered roofs. Carolee Caffrey tells a story from Southern California in which a sister plucked flower petals for the clear and express purpose of dropping them on her brother's head to observe his startled confusion.

Above all, there is one social behavior that is vital and unmissable: crows' irrepressible conversation. "Vocalizes while perched, on the ground, and in flight, while alone or interacting with others," summarizes the *Birds of the World* account. They could have just written: "talks at all times." What do I hear when I hear a calling crow? A bird who speaks to those she knows, her neighbors, parents, sisters, and adopted siblings. In those conversations, I hear a system more familiar than solitude or the flocks of shifting hundreds, and find meanings I can follow.

One afternoon in spring, I step out back among the dumpsters and see a crow perching on a streetlamp: *CAAAW . . . CAAAW . . . CAAAW.* Three long, evenly spaced caws, each given with a theatrically exaggerated lean forward and pump of the tail. A brief look around, and a repeat performance. And in the gaps between bouts I watch and wait, and hear an answering series of three more rough caws from somewhere out of sight. These are territorial declarations, the corvid equivalent of song.

Usually, crows of neighboring families are urged to keep their distance, but such disputes are put on hold when a larger threat appears. One of the clearest and most common calls for clamor is when a predator is discovered: I look up to see three crows cawing in the air above the neighborhood nest, making little dips and dives over a nearby tree. But then more crows flood in and converge on that point, until there are twenty black shapes screaming at the hawk in the canopy's top tier.

On another morning, I'm watching from my window when a crow flies in carrying an enormous piece of bread. It's early and the streets are quiet. She settles on the edge of the pavement and places her burden on the ground. *Caw, caw . . . caw . . . caw . . . caw, caw.* A longer train of notes, quicker and less intense, not with the slow-spaced ceremony of the territorial calls, nor the rough screams of maximum volume to summon all the full county militia. She lowers her head again to her haul and starts to tear and hammer. Two more crows fly in and land beside her, and they all begin to share. These are calls of neither "Neighbor stay away" nor "All crows assemble now," but of "Brother, sister, I've found something!"

How do the crows survive and thrive, here where so many others falter? They are not the biggest or the smallest, not the fastest or most cunningly disguised. But the thing that crows do best is talk, to build the bonds that mean that their beaks are more than one and their eyes are more than two. A great roost of crows mutters in the night like the ocean on the shore or the wind sweeping through a forest. And like the ocean, it can't be silenced, and like the wind, it can't be caught.

A Voice That Speaks to Me

What a delicious sound! It is not merely crow calling
to crow, for it speaks to me too. I am part of one great
creature with him; if he has voice, I have ears. I can hear
when he calls.

—Henry David Thoreau, *The Journal,* January 12, 1855

Like us, crows work together, play together, form long-term bonds, isolate in family groups while making efforts to meet others, and join together when facing outside threats. People often dismiss crows as just another bird, winged and beaked and thoughtless. Correct this false conclusion: count the crows among the thinkers. I love to hear the singing birds, but like us, crows live their lives in prose. They are the second speakers of my town, and everything they do is accompanied by speech. They are our closest social cousins, more like us than other birds. This is not merely an interesting abstraction, but the grounds for our connection. More than any other bird, crows and people interact.

A foundational crow skill, I argued earlier, is their ability to recognize other individuals. Many birds can recognize their mate, but crows might have significant personal memories of twenty birds and passing acquaintance with many more. There is another allied and dramatic difference that sets crows apart: there are no birds more likely to recognize individual humans. (Other corvids are capable of human recognition, but often don't particularly care who we are, whereas crows routinely find us relevant.) The most scientifically well-known example of this was a study at the University of Washington, in which masked researchers visited crow nests to take measurements and band young birds. In the future, they were routinely abused around the college campus if seen wearing the masks.

Conversely, people who regularly feed crows at a particular place will come to be recognized and trusted, and sometimes followed or greeted. There are many anecdotes of regular crow feeders even receiving gifts from their corvid friends. One girl in Seattle was particularly generous with her local crows and received dozens of objects, including buttons, balls, beads, Legos, a broken light bulb, and jewelry. Much as I love the chippies, there is no chance of them bringing me treasures.

Bonds between humans and crows used to be commonplace, rather than newsworthy stories. In the less cautious past, crows were popular pets (now illegal, for reasons I find at least somewhat worthy of reconsideration). Old books are full of stories of pet crows' personality and mischief: caching berries in one owner's shirt pocket (while he was wearing the shirt), perching on a shoulder for companionable preening of their owner's hair, and imitating human phrases and laughter are just a partial anthology. When you've lived with a crow, you don't need studies to tell you that crows can recognize, remember, play, and speak with meaning.

Encounters with wild birds can reveal this too. Crows are always watching, and in each human face look out for potential friends and dangers. Crows are the birds whom we ignore most often, but they are the birds who ignore us least.

I step out into sight, and a junco bursts away to change her sphere of action. Brown birds disregard me from the bushes' edge, and a woodpecker flies to a higher branch to continue feeding without further concern. But the crows keep watching. Some humans are a threat; others may bring gifts or tools. They watch what objects hold my interest, for they use the things we use.

If I leave a garbage bin unclosed or a grocery bag unguarded, then they will be there to investigate in the wake of my departure. In the morning, I fill a birdbath with water, and in the afternoon find submerged in it a piece of no-longer-crusty bread, softening for the crows' consumption. They've long known that our wide, hard roads are good for cracking snail shells, but some items offer more resistance, and more human labor must be harnessed: I ride my bike to work and look up ahead at the sound of a sharp tap on the pavement—a crow has just dropped a walnut taken from a tree we planted and now awaits the sequel. *I'm not going to crack a walnut on my bike, bird. Not as clever as you think!* Then a car comes up behind me, and I hear a crackle under tires.

Falcon watches from the wild, and Coyote from the shadows, but Crow watches from among us to see that the dam he made won't break, to see the work he did to make California safe for people. I know the story has some truth: Crow was here before I came. But I also know how crows live now and that we have returned the favor. Now we are cocreators of the world we share.

To look across a room and find our thoughts reflected in another's glance is an inexhaustible surprise. But look further out and further up. Look across the room, and out the window, and up into the trees and on the rooftops. My eyes move through our human scaffolding, and black eyes return my gaze. A sea of crows is gathering to murmur in the night, and when black arrows streak across the sunset, I understand their call.

CHAPTER 4
WAXWING REVELATIONS

Cedar Waxwing, *Bombycilla cedrorum*

Chippies, squawkers, and crows are all familiar, everyday birds. Cedar waxwings are not. Waxwings are unpredictable and wandering—not everyday birds, but sometimes birds, birds that pop up in my life at unexpected times and places. They don't present the same opportunity for personal familiarity, the way one can come to know and expect the same pair of brown birds to be chipping away outside the window each morning. But the opposites of familiarity are mystery and surprise. Waxwings appear and the week is rescued from uniformity. I hear their secret whistles and the day's staleness floats away.

Their aura of perpetual freshness stems in part from a subtly extravagant appearance. They often seem invisible—it's easy to walk right past waxwings in their quiet, earth-toned softness. Get a good look, however, and they appear theatrically fantastic: thick black bandanas shade their eyes, crests spike upward in angular defiance, and the most undiluted reds and yellows bloom upon their silky feathers. To have ignored them seems implausible. But people, unlike waxwings, are creatures of habit, and tend not to look into the trees each day for rarely present surprises. The reason waxwings remain mysterious to most Californians is that we see them only in winter, when they come down from the north in wandering flocks, searching for berries. A few nest in the uppermost part of the state, but for most of us they are birds that never settle down, seen today and gone tomorrow.

You cannot know all birds in equal detail any more than you can learn all there is to know about every person you encounter. But it takes only the slightest of circumstances—a greeting, a glance—for your imagination to pluck someone from life's endless parade of strangers and invest them with tantalizing possibility. The cedarbirds are such strangers whom I cannot forget.

There are ways to add meaning to the briefest encounters: look more closely, listen more closely, and constantly expect the appearance of indefinable possibilities. If you gather your scattered attention and focus it on the sounds around you and the fleeting forms across the sky, then you will discover that the world contains more birds than you knew. If you practice seeking waxwings, you will find more than what you look for. I watch for the cedarbirds and find that the treetops are not empty. I strain my ears to catch their secret signals and find that the world is never silent.

How to Look

If you position your head within a few feet of a hummingbird feeder, you can watch the bold visitors approach with just the slightest hesitation, close enough to see the rapid extension of their tongue into the liquid and the flaring of their throat feathers when they swivel in irritation at a rival. If you hold still with a handful of sunflower seeds in your hand, the cheekier of human-acclimated chickadees will come to you and pluck them from the channel where your fingers meet. You can't do these things with waxwings. They are not so trusting and self-assured.

So it can be hard to feel in real life as though you are meeting the fantastic cedar waxwings as they are shown in photos. Look at some spectacular image of a whole troop of cavorting marauders with berries in their beaks and they indeed seem like some exotic fantasy of a bird; glance at a living flock, silhouetted and distant in a tree across the street, and you may be hard pressed even to tell what kind of bird they are. But it's important to realize that the photograph is closer to the truth, closer to the full reality, despite the intervening camera. The camera's work lets me imagine those birds immediately before my eyes, as if those berries were living clusters tucked between the pages of my book and a waxwing were perched on the spine, reaching down to pluck them loose. I have never been so close to a living waxwing as in this moment in my mind.

The field guide simply calls them brown. But now I bring my eyes close to this image as if the bird herself were cradled in my hands, and I see the complete inadequacy of the word: her feathers are smooth and pearly with a creamy unblemished luster. On her wings is that strange namesake, that waxy reservoir of accumulated carotenoids that on normal birds are dispersed throughout their feathers but here are built up over years, distilled into a concentrated red that makes handsome house finches appear weakly watered down. Her gray-black tail is tipped in unadulterated yellow, like suncup flowers on a midnight ramble.

Best of all is that face. There is no other songbird with such dramatic sternness and determination inscribed in beak and feathers. This is not to say that this is the waxwings' constant mood, but it is their constant mask: a bold black band across their eyes like the shadowed eye slit of a warrior's helmet, a pointed crest that continues the helmeted motif with belligerent alertness, and a thin white line that extends the division of the downcurved beak into an unyielding scowl.

In some sense, these are mere accidents of plumage that give birds expressions that we read as cute or bumbling, vacuous or grumpy. But accidental or unfair, our instinctive reactions to faces remain. Some people strike us at a glance as dull and unprepossessing, others as warm and welcoming, and then there are those faces that make us simply stop and stare and wonder, with perhaps a discomfiting suspicion that we were ourselves shaped in a very crude and inadequate manner. That's the kind of face that waxwings have. I see that face and forget about carotenoids or subtle traces of sexual dimorphism, forget about evolutionary history or ecological pressures, forget about the ingredients that might make a face like this. I just look and look until the world is just this bird and no longer is mundane.

In principle, you don't need a tour guide to enjoy a sunset, a field of flowers, or such stunning birds as these. In principle, all I need to write to convey my truly simple message is:

Look at them!

W. H. Forbush describes the power of looking at the cedarbirds: "In 1908, some fruit-growers in Vermont introduced into the Assembly a bill framed to allow them to shoot Cedar Waxwings," he narrates. But when the bill proceeded to the upper chamber, "the senators were shown mounted specimens of the bird. That was enough; its beauty conquered and the bill was defeated." To see something with your own eyes outweighs a lot of talk.

Photographs are a good first step in this direction. When photography was younger, taxidermy was the most potent tool we had to get closer to these elusive birds. But now we can do better than pictures in a book or corpses in the Senate chambers; now we can see waxwings as they live and move and speak. The revolutionary tool in this endeavor is a modern pair of binoculars, which I think is rivaled only by the bicycle in its ratio of life enhancement (vast and undiminishing) to lifetime cost (a few hundred dollars for a permanent instrument). Binoculars bestow the ability to see things that are far away as if they were nearby, transforming waxwings twenty yards away to waxwings sitting at your table. Every household should have a pair or two.

I keep binoculars at my desk by the window. Someone is always passing through the trees across the street. A little flash of furtive motion among the drying oak leaves is transformed into a Townsend's warbler, an impossible encapsulated spark of black and yellow. I feel the heft of glass and metal in my hands and enjoy the tactility of a real tool as a relief from the artificial world of screens. I spot a brown smudge moving on the pavement, point myself in its direction, and by a miracle of truly Galilean proportions, what I see through these lenses is not what I saw before, is not what everyone else sees. A smudge becomes a chippie, movement becomes a meeting, and my old friends of the rusty rumps fizz up together from the ground in the volcanic excitement of their mutual rediscovery. What was this without binoculars?

A vital point about binocular ownership: you don't *always* need to use them. Use them to see waxwings well one single time and their image will be imprinted in your memory. You have to get close to someone to establish relations. But once you know that person, a coherent portrait will flash into your mind at the first moment of every subsequent approach. You might next meet waxwings as a dense and distant flock at the limits of your eyesight. But you will spot their red and yellow now that you know they're there, and you will see those masks of black like stepping back into a dream. The deepest purpose of this tool is not to occupy your eyes with a stream of flitting images but to teach your mind the face that you then will always search for.

How to Listen

Despite the inexhaustible fascination of these blacks and reds and yellows, the number of waxwing flocks that I first detect by sight is perhaps one in twenty. When people tell me that they never see waxwings, the problem therefore really seems to be that they don't *hear* waxwings. My most typical waxwing encounter can't be photographed or painted. It sounds like this:

I set off to work on a February morning, pedaling up the hill and gliding down with a rush of wind filling my ears. As I reach the level bottom and that whooshing fades away, I'm suddenly aware of every sound, as if I'd slept all night by a running stream and now walked away into a forest crisp with silence, where a kinglet's slightest sibilance stands out like a single word printed on a wide white page. I hear sounds of people—the zip and resolution of an impact driver, two morning walkers speaking Russian. I hear birds—a white-crowned sparrow with his clear notes and his jumbles, the crows giving the red-shouldered hawk grief. Familiar signals present themselves in sequence; each feels definite and trackable, easily found in space or filed away as a fact. And then there is another sound, a thin, high conversation I can't quite place. Voices slip in and out of empty-seeming air. Someone is whispering in my ears, someone I can't see.

I guess that what I hear are high-pitched lisping whistles, a dozen overlapping voices somewhere in the sky. Some say waxwings speak in trills, or in words like *sree* and *zee*, between a hiss and a buzz. But these are no trills or whistles I can make, or words I can pronounce.

People have "speaking voices" and "singing voices," and these sound more like the latter, raised high above the staff of quotidian conversation. Factually, I know that the waxwings are now speaking in the practical talk of winter and that waxwings in fact don't sing at all—but these are not "speaking voices," not the slow lethargic plodding of the tired everyday. The sparrows are at their most musical this morning and sound like clear sopranos, but this is something else—a jump into a high falsetto, a breathy, airy sound that has the wind still in it.

That's not enough. These voices are still higher than any singer's voice, higher than any ladder I can climb. I purse my lips to their smallest opening, whistle to my highest note, and find myself still octaves short. But if I clamp my jaws together, and then spread my teeth a tiny, subtle distance, invisible in the mirror, then I can hiss and exhale and get a little closer to that voice. High pitch is a tool for evading strangers' ears. For waxwing-level secrecy, merely opening my mouth is to commit an indiscretion.

I guess the closest thing I can think of is no human sound at all. I heard it yesterday and started scanning through the treetops for the cedarbirds, but it was just the squeaky braking of a car, brief little stop-and-start squeals of hesitant reversing down a slope. But that comparison is too heavy with machinery and metal—it's as if those lisping squeaks had grown tired of their clumsy car and clumsy driver, and each one had taken off in sequence as it sounded, rising from the rubbing rotor to join a little flock now circling the neighborhood.

My thinking mind intrudes to remind me that what I hear is still conversation and has its practical purposes. These are words like other contact calls, the keep-in-touch notes of birds, but made for birds in flight. The chippies speak in well-spaced and resonant chirps, adequate for birds moving slowly and at a distance from their partner. But the waxwings are often flying when they speak, undulating in a tight flock across the sky, so their conversation is quiet but constant, overlapping and uninterrupted, to keep them tied together.

My thinking mind reminds me that there is a reason why these calls are so hard to hear—I know that these are secret signals, evolved to evade finer senses than mine. I've read how other birds, like the sparrows and the robins on this same block, have developed high-pitched alarm calls because they are difficult for predators to locate. The sky remains resolutely empty as I search its expanse and listen, but I needn't feel too bad. A Cooper's hawk perches in the tree, looks up, and like me wonders where that sound can come from.

And now it seems to me that the highness of those calls and the highness of that flight are both invitations that lift my mind above the pavement. This speech falls on the border of my physical ability to hear. A little higher in the spectrum, and I would hear nothing and live in ignorance of the waxwings all around me. A little lower, and it would grow mundane like other sounds. But as it is, they speak to my ears only when I am at my most attentive. Waxwings constantly remind me of the limits of perception as we practice it, remind me that what we see and hear in our everyday lives is just a fragment of reality, but that we can choose to access more.

My pedaling has ceased as I slow and listen, stop and look, look and fail to find. I hear that sound as it trails off into the distance, and smile that they have eluded me again. I am glad for that alpine quietness, lost in the spread of blue above. The consequence of waxwings' whispering is that I listen to every word. The paradox of these birds that most make me pay attention is that I never saw them.

Where to Seek Them

People often ask me where they should go to see waxwings. They want an address, a specific park they can go to at a specific time. This approach works for many birds, which are often stunning examples of philopatry, the love of home that keeps them in one place despite incredible natural mobility. It doesn't work for waxwings. Like other birds, waxwings are capable of distance-devouring flight, physically free to wander where they will. Unlike most other birds, they actually do.

"My only country is the sea," goes the "Canción del pirata" of José de Espronceda. Waxwings' homeland is likewise wherever they find their unpredictable sustenance on the wild and trackless continent. There is a significant seasonal movement along the lines that one would expect, with an exodus from the north in winter. But the extent and exact direction of that movement varies every year depending on the fluctuating berry crops they find. For most of California, waxwings are winter birds, but whether they will be most numerous in my neighborhood this year in November, January, or April, I really couldn't say.

All that can be said with certainty is that where there are waxwings, there are berries. In winter they eat essentially nothing else, adding a dash of flowers and invertebrates in spring. Their name acknowledges their taste for the fruits of the eastern cedar, a kind of juniper, while the old New England name of "cherry-bird" likewise commemorates a favorite food (and the reason for the Vermont fruit-growers' vendetta). Here in California, I might go for a walk in the woods in fall and find them devouring the lingering madrone berries, their silky faces nearly hidden by those silvered and unfalling leaves as their shrill, high voices crackle in the cool and songless air. I might stroll down my street and into town on a warming day of early spring and be surprised to confront them right before my eyes in some modest planted pistache or plane, seeming more discreet than ever as the linnets and the juncos sing.

Some people find such unpredictability frustrating. I like it. I've never been a fan of the school of watching birds based around the pursuit of definite objectives, where success means checking something off a list. Lists are tedious things for groceries and obligations. But waxwings can't be bought, scheduled, or complained about. The only rational expectation on any given day is "probably no waxwings," or perhaps a more positive but accommodating "I'll see something or other."

That's the pleasure of waxwing unpredictability on a daily basis—hey, there they are! But on a broader scale of months and years, such regular unpredictability does form some level of expectation. I know I'll find them sometime, even if not today. What unpredictability teaches in the long run is comfort in the zone of expectant patience. Unhurried alertness is the attitude that is most fruitful for finding waxwings, and is also the attitude that will deliver the most fruitful attention to life's many birds and other pleasures. When searching for the cedarbirds, patience is better than a map.

So if you grow weary of looking up into the trees with disappointed eyes, just recall the Bombycilline Catechism:

Where can I find waxwings?
You can find them here.

When will I find them?
What's your hurry?

Your grip thus tightened on your credo, off you go into the world, ready for whatever pops up. Take it slow. Look for berries. Waxwings might well eat them, sooner or later. You probably won't see them today, and that is fine. That is good and proper to their nature as wild, wandering animals. Wildness is what we're looking for, not tame predictability.

If you don't see any waxwings today, that is good. The single most important skill for bringing more birds into your life is the ability to wait patiently and receptively. Some people see hundreds of birds each day, and some people don't see any, though they live on the same street. The biggest difference clearly isn't the quality of their binoculars or the physical acuity of their hearing—it's what they pay attention to.

Are waxwings absent from your life? Step out your door and step down the street, with your eyes and ears wide open. Last night, the golden-crowned sparrows arrived to sing their waterfall refrain. Tomorrow February ends, and a robin will chant his springtime song. And somewhere, now, the cedarbirds are on the wing and whisper in the clouds. Today may be the day when bare branches bud and burst with the black-masked wanderers of winter. Today the air will shake and shimmer with their high and seething whistles.

CHAPTER 5
DAWN'S WATCHER

American Robin, *Turdus migratorius*

There is a song in darkness that promises the day.

As far as human eyes can tell, the spring sky is still lit by stars alone when the robins start to sing. But those who watch the horizon before dawn may see a morning star, and those who listen at night's closing will hear the sun before they see it. There is a light too faint for our daytime eyes to see, but thrushes are crepuscular and see best in the amber in-betweens. That faintest light is what they wait for, the cue to end their silence.

Deedle-eee! Dee-dum. Di-dee! The voice rises and falls in wave after wave, rolling unseen from the treetops. Another robin across the street makes a competing claim. His words are a little different, but the pattern is the same: rising and falling, rising and falling, and the rising phrases seem more pronounced and eager, as if each step downward were just a preparation for a leap, a spring's compression before a new expansion.

Maybe in daylight this would sound like just another singing bird, but in this earliest of overtures, the robins' unchallenged chorus seems magnified and grander. The world and all its things to do are dormant and unreal. The sky is dark and humans rest, but these singers have decided that the time for sleep is over.

The songs rise and fall, up and down in pitch. Each downward step is a tiny pause, and each longer pause between the verses is a moment in which to catch one's breath. The robins pull and rest, like sailors heaving on a rope to raise an anchor from the ocean. They pull and rest, and the sun is tied to the end of the line. They raise the light from the darkest sea until all the birds are singing.

The Trees Are No Longer Full of Strangers

To understand the meaning of a bird's song, you first have to recognize it and tie it to its author. Robins are perfect birds to teach this skill, singing widely and vigorously throughout the state and across the continent. They are especially known for singing at dawn and twilight, filling up the air while other birds are waking up or falling silent.

It helps that robins are familiar and abundant birds overall—it's no struggle to find them for practice. They are relatively large members of the thrush family, the size of plump jays with reddish breasts and gray backs, a little more boldly contrasting in males than in the paler females. Suburbanites often know them as runners across lawns who stop from time to time to cock their heads and look for worms moving beneath the surface.

In California, their breeding (and therefore singing) range was formerly restricted to summer-moist areas like Sierran meadows and the northwestern coastal fog zone, where they could find mud for nest construction and pluck worms and other invertebrates from the soft soil. In winter, they would spread out through the lowlands, roaming like waxwings between berry-bearing trees, and they still do this today, from the wild toyons to the sidewalk-splitting camphors. But with the spread of irrigation for agriculture and urban landscaping, robins now nest in most settled areas of California. Summer drought is a defining feature of our state's historical ecology; summer irrigation is a defining feature of our contemporary urban, suburban, and agricultural landscape. The song of springtime robins is the sound of watered California.

Now we have constant opportunities to hear them. The first goal is simply to recognize a robin when you hear one singing, and there are specific techniques to make this easier. The object is to translate abstract sounds into forms you can remember, using methods that will help you as you turn to other birds. Return to these suggestions with a recording you can play while you train these different ways of thinking—this practice is where I always start when I want to get closer to a bird. I don't think there's any way around it: you have to actually listen as you work with each of these techniques. You can't learn music by reading a book in silence. The best-written program notes or detailed analyses of a composer's intentions won't do you any good if you can't tell a violin from a clarinet.

Method 1: Mnemonic phrases, memorable but imprecise. The use of English words to approximate a bird's vocalization gives us a meaning we can hold on to more naturally and easily, especially when the chosen words align with our emotional impression or the function of the sound. Many common birds already have traditional mnemonics, or you can make up your own. For robin song, the classic rendering is something along the lines of "cheerily, cheer-up, cheerio."

The audible resemblance is that the song is made up of series of short musical phrases of usually two (cheer-up) or three syllables (cheer-i-o). Play your recording and mentally overlay a string of "cheerios" and "cheer-ups." The effectiveness of the phrase as a memory device is that it evokes the sense of cheerful, optimistic vigor that many people hear in this bird's voice. Have you ever heard Louis Armstrong sing "Red, Red Robin"? The song elaborates on the same idea, cadence, and phrasing:

> Wake up, wake up, you sleepy head
>
> Get up, get up, get out of bed,
>
> Cheer up, cheer up, the sun is red
>
> Live, love, laugh and be happy!

If a message of "wake up, get up, cheer up" becomes your automatic mental transcription when you hear a singing robin, then reliable recognition has been achieved.

Method 2: Transliteration, more exact, but less memorable. If you are more literal minded and resist attributing cheerfulness and loving laughter to robins, you can instead attempt the closest transliteration possible with our letters while avoiding the superfluous meanings of our words. I might come up with something along the lines of "deedle-dee, dee-dum, dee-di" or borrow a Spanish rendition of "piwío, pihi, piwó" from Héctor Gómez de Silva to avoid all tint of English meaning. Remember, the effectiveness of such an approach is entirely dependent on finding a combination of letters you can hear in your head as you hear the song; such transliterations are not meant to stand alone as complete reproductions of these complex strings of sounds, but are just a shorthand to help you file away these songs in your *verbal* memory, where it is easier for us language-adapted humans to find them again.

Method 3: Description, as exact and memorable as you are capable of putting into words. Some songs call for a more external approach, not reproducing the sound, but walking around it, looking at it from different angles of pitch, tone, and tempo. You might employ musical terminology, everyday adjectives, or memorable analogies. In this fashion, I would describe the robin's song as multiple series of four or more medium-low-pitched phrases of two to three syllables each. The tone is generally clear, loud, and liquid, with a kind of vigorous, annunciatory brightness that some find evoked by the word *caroling*. Robin songs also sometimes end their series of "cheerio" phrases with a higher-pitched, more complex phrase transcribable as "hissely" or describable with adjectives including *throaty*, *strangled*, or *whispered*.

To learn this for yourself, play the song repeatedly and try to hear each element of this description. If you dissent from my vocabulary and would propose different adjectives, then do so! Stick to the words that stick to you.

Method 4: Sonograms, the most exact approach, but generally requiring some practice for intuitive and memorable use. Visual renditions of sounds reveal details that are otherwise very hard to distinguish. Consider this robin song:

This is what four unique "cheerio" phrases look like on the page, each made up of two or three pitches in different arrangements and transitions (a high note slurring downward, then jumping partway back up; a slightly wavering note with a little bump up at the end; slurring up to a high note, then dropping down; medium-low-high). Each robin has a repertoire of ten to twenty different caroling phrases, particular "cheer-ups" and "cheerios" that he repeats at intervals, and it is possible to pick them out. A single "cheerio" passes very quickly, and it is initially difficult to discern three separate pitches. But you can see them on the page and know that they are there: play a song while following a sonogram until you can trace the rapid ups and downs within each phrase. The first goal here is simple: to recognize that this song is made up of discrete words or musical motifs, rather than an uninterrupted flow of random sound. After you've spent some time in the sustained attentiveness that sonogram-tracking demands, it will be hard to confuse the robin's song with others.

Be patient as you practice this new language. Listening like this is like close-reading a poem or working your way through a piano passage figuring out the underlying chords and the best fingering. Maybe you will spend thirty minutes as you play and replay a few recordings, consciously tracing out these different perspectives before crossing your threshold one morning to hear the musician performing outside your door.

All songs must have a singer to share their richest meaning. Words are not self-sufficient, with their significance and luster contained within mere letters—we're always looking for the author back behind them somewhere. Imagine picking up a ringing phone with no knowledge of the caller, and then hearing a voice that's dear to you. If someone asked you why you smiled at that unemotive word "Hello," how would you explain it? By the simple warmth of recognition: "I knew him instantly."

That is your goal with birds.

The First Message of the Singers: Territory

Recognition is itself an invaluable enrichment of your life. To find the formerly indefinite muddle of the world now populated with familiar individuals makes it much more intelligible and interesting. But birdsong, of course, does not exist primarily for the convenient aural survey of species by humans. Recognizing *who* is singing is the prologue to recognizing *why* he's singing.

There is a general consensus that there are two main evolutionary reasons for birdsong: territorial declaration and courtship. Territories first.

Among the various breeding systems you see among North American songbirds, one of the most common is seasonal monogamy, in which a single male bird and a single female bird join together for a spring and summer to raise their young, while excluding others of their species from their nesting territory. This is what robins do, typically returning to the same general breeding area and so sometimes reconnecting with the same partner, but not actively maintaining a multiyear bond with their mate. (Permanent Nations of Two are not the avian norm.)

In such a system, a key concept to understand is that of territory, a core defended area that birds—especially adult males—consider generally off-limits to those beyond their immediate family. Maintaining a private territory can be a way of defending access to food resources, and some species maintain territories all year round. But the majority of songbirds, robins included, defend territories only during the breeding season, when the jealous imperatives of monogamy are in full swing. It is widely considered more offensive for a stranger to intrude on one's wife than on one's pantry. The main evolutionary purpose of territory is to ensure genetic paternity.

What does it mean to "defend a territory"? It can and does entail actual physical chases and fighting. But the more intense the combat gets, the higher both the potential dangers and inevitable expenditures of energy are. If you are a younger or weaker male robin with no territory of your own, it is not in your interest to go around picking fights with all the stronger territory holders. This is where song comes in as a key element of territorial display. Birds sing from prominent perches, often near the borders of their territory, to ensure that neighbors know of the presence of a breeding male. Such songs may also, by their duration and force-fulness, communicate signals of the singer's health and vigor. More often than not, singing prevents the need to fight, because it is easier for all parties concerned to simply respect the border.

Robins in California offer a perfect demonstration of spring's establishment of territory and the sonic reflection of that shift in seasons. In spring, robins defend territories and sing to tell others to keep their distance. In winter, robins flock and chatter in cooperation. Their seasonal changes are exceptionally clear both to see and to hear.

Some people think of robins as birds of spring. That's true in Maine. Here it's not. In most of inhabited California, we have more robins in winter, when breeding birds from the north or from the mountains descend in flocks to the lowlands. I've often found myself on some January day, watching a seemingly inexhaustible flow of robins pouring out of a tree and into the sky, bird after bird, over a hundred. That doesn't happen in spring, when flocks break apart.

In winter, I like to visit my parents' house at the other end of town, because they have a pond on the edge of their neighborhood that fills up with goldeneyes, pretty ducks that do wonderfully bizarre courtship yoga as the season moves along. And from their house I'll stroll through the neighborhood, richly planted with berry-bearing Chinese pistache and camphor trees, along with the usual scatterings of pyracanthas and privets and who knows what other fruit-laden ornamentals. Sometimes I'll meet waxwings. I'll nearly always hear robins.

They can be hidden in the leaves above the sidewalk, but from that tree comes a steady stream of whinnies, brief explosive trills that sound like bursts of unwilling laughter as provoked by merciless tickling. I can hear them from down the street. As I draw near to the invisible laughers, the propulsive chortles turn to a tensely anticipatory clucking—before, they were jostling among themselves, but now the robins are giving cautious warnings of a threat on the ground. Now I'm right underneath, and a few sharp, piercing "cheep!" notes ring out as the birds that were exposed on the lower branches hop up and overhead. There might be thirty robins in this tree, but even with my binos focused on the foliage, I catch only furtive glimpses of three or four. I couldn't see them, and many of them couldn't see me—but they changed their behavior, speech, and position because someone saw me and spoke up. Winter robins communicate and work together.

When spring arrives, those conversations grow thin, a few words between flockless pairs drowned out by the loud carols of their songs. Now I step out before dawn when it's still too dark to feed or fight, and already they're beginning: a robin climbs the tallest redwood in the neighborhood to launch his song. A voice replies across the street and a third three houses down. I send my ears out into the distance, and they find other robins beginning their daily contest. Before, there were dozens of robins perched in a single tree. Now there is just a handful on the street, and each one is declaring his own piece of the earth. "Territorial display" is not a bookish and theoretical conception: it's plain to see and hear. In winter, I heard an orderly discussion of thirty cautious, muted voices, but in the same place in spring, I hear three proud, possessive males, each waking up and stepping forth to shout to the whole neighborhood—"Stay off my lawn!"

In spring, the amity of winter splinters as each individual swells up with private pride. Birds sing not in harmony but competition. People think of singing birds and hear the joyful, lovesick, or lonely. Each term may have in certain cases elements of truth. But most widespread is jealousy and intolerance of trespass, even before the females come.

The Second Message of the Singers: Courtship

The second function of song is courtship, the variable assemblage of behaviors male birds engage in to convince potential mates of their quality. Often, the territorial functions of song serve as an indirect, preliminary stage in that endeavor: as with many migratory songbirds, unmated male robins will often claim a territory through song and physical defense and then await the arrival of a female with that geographical proof of status as a main theme of their resume. With an emphasis that varies by species, females may also evaluate males based on several other qualities, including plumage, aggression and athleticism, or prospective parental responsiveness.

But song is one of the most common demonstrations of male fitness among songbirds, not just as a preliminary tool for establishing a territory, but as a convincing proof in itself. Song can reveal a bird's physical and mental health, intelligence, nutritional status, and implicit aptitude at foraging. A robin who is weak and undernourished, generally dull witted, and barely scraping by will not sing vigorous and inventive songs, exposing himself to predators and taking hours out from feeding time. Song is not mere *telling*, not mere words and boasting, but *showing*—high-quality song cannot easily be replicated by the less capable.

If an important part of song's message is a declaration of vibrant health, can we make any allied statements about a singing bird's state of mind? One of the most commonly encountered presuppositions is that singing birds are happy. I think the main ingredient in that supposition is not a carefully articulated theory of avian cognition but a direct emotional reaction based on our human experience of birdsong's setting and musical impression. I admit it too—I often do feel happy on a fine spring morning full of robin song. The robin song *does* sound cheerful.

Cheer up, cheer up, the sun is red

Live, love, laugh and be happy!

Human perception finds many bird songs suggestive of jubilant enthusiasm for life. This is fuzzy and incomplete, but not entirely divorced from reality. Birds do not sing in blithe and carefree happiness, but they do sing in strength, vigor, and unruminative confidence. The truth of birdsong is much closer to excited eagerness than to the melancholy we hear in exceptional cases such as golden-crowned sparrows or hermit thrushes. Wistful melancholy can sound beautiful to us—but it is a highly misleading label to apply to the probable emotions of the bird. If you wanted to select a species whose song sounds like what birdsong "really means," whose audible impression on humans aligns with our best guess at its audible impression on birds, whose song sounds *to us as well* like confident strength and vigorous eagerness for any challenge, then the robin would be an excellent nomination.

The "Red, Red Robin" lyrics are not entirely wrong, but the trumpet's voice that follows comes a good deal closer. I think there is valuable truth in Thoreau's description of the robin:

It sings with power, like a bird of great faith that sees the bright future through the dark present. . . . They are sounds to make a dying man live.

Strength, vigor, and confidence are valid, authentic, and crucial messages for courtship song. To sing with power and faith is not an accident but a biological intention.

Song is the opposite of hesitation, is impatient and must speak. Song is the opposite of caution, that outworn winter prudence. There was a time when it seemed wise to hide, to be merely one of the timid flock. Now is when each robin must show himself strong enough to stand alone.

The Reflection of a Star

Spring's dawn chorus is the most magical of moments. I love to picture in my mind the turning of the earth, the line of sunlight sweeping westward across the continent. As that border of illumination approaches and culminates, the silence of the night is broken by a sudden crescendo from the birds, a wave that rises and recedes in a continuous cycle around the planet.

I go outside in the darkness of the quiet early hours, before the day catches me in its chains. I'm out before the workers and the walkers, out before the crows and brown birds, and out before the sun. The earth revolves, and I am carried with it—not standing still but spinning, turning to face a star so much closer than the others. The next town over has already met that line of light, and now I am swept toward it. I look to the east and can see nothing yet. But the robins are dawn's watchers, and in the deep dark of their eyes a faintest glimmer is reflected. They see a star I cannot see, and it draws their music from them like a flower from the earth.

I hear that song that I have studied and recognize its author in his carols and his whispers. I hear that the flock of winter has dissolved into a dozen separate kingdoms. I hear that each singer seeks his queen, the pale listener who gathers sticks and mud and shapes them with her body into a grass-lined cradle.

These are the profound essentials of hearing birds in spring: recognition, territory, courtship. There are more acts to follow and variations on these themes. But Robin sings the overture and you hear the curtain rise.

CHAPTER 6
THE BLESSED HALO

House Finch, *Haemorhous mexicanus*

We have a tendency to overlook quite wonderful things, once they grow familiar. Birds are one of the most obvious of all examples of this: we are surrounded by flying, singing capsules of life feathered in red and gold—and we ignore them. If we had no birds in our lives and only read about them in stories, we would think them appropriately fantastic characters for myths and legends. But our lives are full of birds, so we rarely think of them at all.

You can decide, however, to reenchant your life. You can choose to peel away that concealing layer of quotidian gray and rediscover the brilliant core that's been present all along. Select a bird that embodies those fundamental avian splendors of flight, song, and color and imagine you are seeing and hearing it for the first time in your life. The house finch, or California linnet, is just such a bird. But it is another species highly subject to that ruthless diminisher of human interest known as Ubiquity, and so it often goes underappreciated.

Embrace the common. Abundance is a great mark in a bird's favor. You need go nowhere to see wonders. Dawson considered this red presence in his life a cause for constant gratitude:

> The linnet is the bread-and-butter of the bird feast which life
> daily spreads before us. . . . The home that is not surrounded
> by an investing halo of linnets, I hold it to be unblest.

Look again: your home, your street, your corner park are blessed. These neighbors invite you daily to a feast no matter your preoccupations. If you are beset by a million little things demanding your attention, step outside and leave them. There is a halo around your home, a wreath of singing scarlet. Walk within that cloud of song, and both worries and stale temptations lose their urgency and luster. Your hunger for the novel will be sated when you find the feast that never ends.

Linnets and Californians Go Together

Picture a bird feeder, some simple tray well stocked with sunflower seeds. The matte black shells are ridged with sturdy little arches to protect the latent life from insects and moisture. But a familiar bird arrives, a little smaller than a sparrow, lighter and more nimble, and from her the seeds have no defense. She is a discreet maternal color, a streaky mix of pale and brownish-gray, well suited to sit on an open nest and draw no undesired attention. Her mate flies in, the same in size and shape, but suffused with red that glows on his forehead and runs all through his breast. Each seizes on a seed, and the two halves of their stocky beaks grind together until the broken shells fall empty to the side. Even the plainest everyday birds have their special niche and skill: few can match the linnets' beaks when it comes to hulling seeds.

If you know this bird, you probably know it as the house finch. Which is a perfectly reasonable name that points out this bird's proclivity for human proximity, her comfort and familiarity under our eaves and in our gardens. But it's actually quite a modern coinage, a name based on a few scant decades of domestic cohabitation. The old books call them linnets, due to their similarity and relation to the linnets of the Old World, the birds of Wordsworth and Tennyson and several centuries of this language that we speak here now. How did Yeats envision the refuge that he kept in his "deep heart's core"? He saw the Lake Isle of Innisfree, where "midnight's all a glimmer, and noon a purple glow / And evening full of the linnet's wings."

And so the most esteemed poets of California continue to opt for this term of address, as do the old English ladies who come into my nature shop. Gary Snyder describes a scene of the Sierras in which "linnets crack seeds at the feed tray," and Robert Hass is struck by that most vivid red of the California skyscape when he sees the air full of "linnets like wounds." Would you like to be a poet too, someone whose words are charged with meaning, who sees the world not in dull prose but in endless chains of image, metaphor, and memory? Offer some sunflower seeds to the linnets and watch them. All the material you need is there.

And that material is easy to find. Ubiquity is no defect, but rather the linnet's most outstanding characteristic. They are abundant in suburban neighborhoods and fairly ready colonizers of the truly urban, lagging only a few birds such as house sparrows and pigeons in their tolerance for sparsely vegetated concrete. Hang up that tray of sunflower and it will be the rare offering that does not find house finch favor within the week.

Birds can be excluded from certain habitats by an absence of appropriate food or by a scarcity of nesting sites. Linnets overcome the first challenge thanks to their flexibility, eating seeds of all types along with a smattering of insects, fruit, and leafy greens. They navigate the second through a similar lack of prejudice when it comes to fitting housing for their budding families. A modest ornamental tree or shrub will suffice to hold their little cup of grasses, as will a ledge under the eave, a wreath on the door, a patio lamp fixed to the wall, or a hanging potted plant (those are a particular favorite). Anything that lifts their children above the dangers of the ground will satisfy their unparticular requirements.

In the East, linnets have even taken to squeezing into enclosed birdhouses, which our finches here don't do. Those eastern house finches are a rather odd branch of the family. Historically, this is a western bird, with some old books even calling them "California linnets," since we are, along with the southwestern states, the true heart of their domain. But if you didn't have house finches in your life, you would want them—a fact worth remembering when we dismiss the all-too-common. So pet dealers brought them east, finding ready customers for even caged and captive "Hollywood finches." When a number of these birds were released in New York in 1939, they quickly adapted to their new setting and grew from that small introduced population to cover most of the eastern half of the country, where they did not previously occur.

Such introductions often have unintended consequences. In this case, there were two of ecological significance. One was that this new house finch population displaced the related purple finch from some areas. Another was that the low genetic diversity of the eastern population made it vulnerable to disease, especially a form of conjunctivitis sometimes known as "house finch eye disease." For a time in the 1990s, it seemed as though the majority of eastern house finches suffered from this sickness, which causes crusty swellings over the eyes that lead to partial or complete blindness, often succeeded by starvation, vulnerability to predators, or other fatal terminations.

The disease has since moderated from those extremes, after a crash in eastern populations, but it continues to be seen regularly, now across the entirety of the country. If you observe linnets on a daily basis, you will inevitably encounter its traces. Usually, there is little to be done: unless the disease is far advanced, birds will remain active and unwilling to be caught for treatment. Some people choose to take down bird feeders when they see its symptoms, in an attempt to reduce crowding and contact, but the birds are social in all settings, and a reliable food source can be a helpful aid to natural recovery. Feeding stations are in fact the source of most of our observations and knowledge of this disease and so seem on balance more helpful than harmful. Keep your feeders clean, but know that the existence of this disease is not your fault.

Today many nationalized field guides elide this bifurcated regional history: you see one big map and are left to assume that the birds live where they have always lived. But before the pet dealers' linnet grab, there were few birds more distinctly typical of our state. "Without question the most abundant bird in California," Dawson declared them in 1923. "So familiar and abundant through parts of California that Red-head and his wife are often regarded as a nuisance," summed up William Finley from a national perspective in a 1917 *Birds of America*. Mary Austin moved to the California desert and was struck by the overflowing abundance of "linnet time" in her 1903 classic, *The Land of Little Rain*:

> Young linnets grow out of the rabbit-brush in the night. All the nests discoverable in the neighboring orchards will not account for the number of them. Somewhere, by the same secret process by which the field matures a million more seeds than it needs, it is maturing red-hooded linnets for their devouring.

California is where the linnets belong. Here they need no cages to bring song into your home. Even further: the linnets feel they belong in your very backyard, accepting your household structures as a useful gift on which to lay their eggs and raise their young. Many animals feel they belong far from human habitation, or perhaps that *we* do not belong in what was previously their home. But for house finches more than for the great majority of birds, human cohabitation is natural and instinctively desirable.

Between study at Berkeley and trail work in the Sierra Nevada, Snyder translated the poems of Chinese poet Han Shan. When asked for directions to his mountain home, Snyder's hermit evasively replies that there is only one way to reach Cold Mountain:

> If your heart was like mine
> You'd get it and be right here.

This is the California linnet. She and I chose the same place for our home, and neither of us needs to ask the way.

The Scarlet and the Music

Imagine for a moment that linnets were not so familiar. Imagine that they were like some less common brilliant bird, a tanager or bunting, that we are always excited to encounter. If linnets made such intermittent appearances, I suspect they would attract a similar regard. We remember and seek out the yellow, orange, and blue birds, admiring their colors. We forget: these too-familiar linnets are our reddest birds. True, they are no shocking cardinal crimson. But California never wears the deciduous splendor of an autumn in New England, so when the poison oak leaves light up in scarlet, I drop such futile comparisons and consider the scene before my eyes. There are many shades of red, and each one is vividly itself.

"Linnets like wounds," Hass wrote. That is the best description of the classic house finch red, the red that spills from the male's forehead to flow downward, as blood does—brightly staining the throat and breast before gradually growing faint on the belly and leaving the back and wings untouched. The wound is frontal, with the exception of a red rump patch seen when they fly (*Haemorhous* means "blood-rumped"). Peterson famously described their relatives the purple finches as looking like "sparrows dipped in raspberry juice." The house finch red is not so gentle, not so much a soft suffusion uniformly absorbed on the upperparts as an aggressive spreading stain that stands out by its contrast with the gray-brown on the side of the head and on the wings.

At a distance, linnets dot their sanguine paint on the landscape, rents and tears in an otherwise unpunctured scene of tranquil greens and browns. If your backyard was a painting by Turner or Cézanne, then that linnet, that little smudge of stand-out red, would be the most interesting thing on the canvas. So if that image framed within your window seems flat and old and ugly, abstract yourself from reality a little, squint your eyes into an impressionistic filter of our oversharp existence, and watch them turn from mundane birds into the peppery dashes of color that enliven the whole scene.

I should also clarify—to instill some trace of natural history in this tale of painters' palettes—that the house finch red is subject to variation. Some plumage colors are consistently created through internal means, but there are other pigments derived from compounds found only in certain food sources. In linnets, the consequence of this latter means of color production is that the exact tint of red is determined by the individual bird's diet at the time of feather growth. While there is indeed a textbook bloody red for house finches, it is also normal to see some birds that are distinctly toward the apricot end of the spectrum. Such departures from a properly balanced diet can be temporarily detrimental to a bird's mating success, as females select for the healthiest males as evidenced by lustrous redness.

The second obvious domain in which birds compete for female approval is of course song. These two traits demonstrate fitness both directly (since genetic or dietary deficiencies are revealed) and implicitly, because they involve the bearer expending his time or energy in making himself more conspicuous to predators and the world at large. Evident thriving despite this self-imposed handicap indicates overflowing, vigorous health. Color and song make birds stand out and grab our attention too, because such attention grabbing is the essential heart of their whole purpose.

The song of linnets seems to grab me on every springtime street. It reaches through my open windows and wraps me in its cloud of sound each time I step outside my doorway. I go to work, and when at intervals I poke my head into the parking lot, it greets me there as well, hanging in the air like a tantalizing curry cooking, until at last I count the cash and close up shop and emerge to find the table set. Then I breathe in the sound of linnets, the most pungent ingredient in the air of spring.

What does it sound like? The main currents are composed of warmly bubbling warbles, rapid runs of different notes too fast to count or separate. Each male has his repertoire of half a dozen songs or so, and sometimes if I listen closely, I can hear when a bird repeats a favored tune two times in quick succession. Most of the finches—and several other birds—have songs that could similarly be classed as cheerful warbles, but the linnet has a special closing tag to help you hear him: he often ends his phrases with a loud, buzzy *veeeer!* that slurs upward like a long zipper accelerating to its zipped-up consummation. The song rambles on for a few pleasant seconds and then dispels your doubts as to its author: *tayo tayo tatitata teeyee teetoo titi ti-VEEEER!*

What does it *feel* like? It's quite popular to preface "warble" with some adjective of uniform good spirits such as "cheerful" or "joyous." (I've yet to see a bird book employ the phrase "despondent warble.") In general, a sense of excitement and enthusiasm seems to be our natural impression from any string of loud, quick notes given on a bright spring day. But the linnet song is even cheerier than the average. Maybe its medium pitch feels richer and more relatable than thinner, higher-pitched voices; maybe those ending upslurred buzzes add a flavor of rambunctiousness inexpressible through more conventional pretty whistles alone. As the irrepressibly enthusiastic Berkeley poet Charles Keeler put it in 1899: "I know of no bird which, if its song be a true guide, has a lighter and more exuberant heart. There is much of the freedom and nonchalance of unrestrained delight in its tones."

Keeler is of course quite out of date. As strict biology, his account ranges from flatly wrong ("nonchalance") or largely wrong ("unrestrained delight") to roughly correct ("exuberant") and endlessly debatable ("freedom"). But when it comes to the musical impression given by house finch song, I have to admit that he has captured my typical mood when waltzing down a linnet-lined street in liberty and lighthearted independence. There are advantages to not being constantly constrained by scientific propriety in one's listening to birds: Keeler had the finch's song inscribed indelibly in his imagination, and he found hearing it to be a source of inexhaustible refreshment.

We don't hear what the linnets hear, and in the end we can't. We make our best guesses as to the role of song in the lives of birds and integrate those theories with our observations to draw more complete and coherent portraits. But we also hear music with tones that they did not intend, and I see no compelling reason for the development of scientific awareness to take that pleasure from us. There are two separate songs, that which the linnet sings and that which humans hear. The first one gives me insight, better understanding, and a certain respectability as a conscientious observer of scientific objectivity. The second gives me joy.

The Reenchantment of the World
Begins at Home

I look up into the trees that line my downtown street and see bodies, red and brown, that are animated and alive, half hidden in the leaves. I forget the cars and passing conversations as I hear a woodwind warble rise above them. Suddenly the birds take flight with a few mellow notes of coordination, and I watch those living tufts of feathers dip and rise into the blue. To be light enough to fly is to feel the density of air under your wings as we might swim in water. The breeze brushes over my face, and I try to taste the subtle currents that those weightless flyers know.

If you wish to reenchant your surroundings, to enter into myths and stories with a mere step outside your door, then song and color and birds are the way to do so. Believe like Hass in "the magic of names and poems." Be glad your world has reds and blues and yellows that fly across the sky in a swelling cloud of music. This is no abstract nature worship, no embrace of nostalgia or fuzzy thinking over the hard realities of science, but simply a more vivid awareness of the world that you can see and hear today.

I went on a fine adventure yesterday: across the parking lot, between the cars, past the chain coffee shop and shoe store to the mailbox, which was full of ads and bills. But I stepped out of my doorway and saw a nest where a shy brown head peeked out. I walked across the pavement and saw four red scars flying across an unhurt sky. And on the roof and neon signs, in the lattice with tired paint and in the shallow-planted trees, from a dozen different points across that sea of asphalt and machines, I heard the warbles rising in unrestrained delight.

If your years have passed in silence and the skies seem lifeless, dull, and barren, look out and look again. Red spills over these dry hills, and melodies burst upward like a thousand popping corks. Just listen to the linnets and let the scarlet halo cast its spell.

CHAPTER 7
THIS GOLDFINCH IS NOT LESSER

Lesser Goldfinch, *Spinus psaltria*

Tiny, gold, and garrulous—this is the California prodigy that the modern books miscall the lesser goldfinch. If you've seen a group of little yellow birds eating seeds at a feeder, then you have likely made their acquaintance and perhaps begun to question that unimpressive appellation.

Maybe you've seen them plucking flowers from the January oaks or unlocking seeds from the woody safes of alders, heard their high and plaintive whistles sounding from the treetops. Maybe you've seen a flock float over a meadow, pausing for a moment on the thinnest spires of the grasses. Even those insubstantial perches barely dip upon their landing. Then they flutter off, green backed and blinking wings of white, quietly coordinating with soft staccato calls. Almost everywhere you go, California's greens and browns are dotted with these ornaments of gold.

And if you've seen and heard them, maybe then you know: this goldfinch is not lesser. The name was given as a marker of that insignificant comparison of size, smaller as they are than the wider-ranging American goldfinch. But I will admit descriptions only in the superlative degree: the bird the old books call the green-backed goldfinch is the most tolerant and agreeable, the most unfailingly brilliant, and the most musically virtuosic of all our California neighbors.

The Fruit of Agreeableness Is Overflowing Abundance

Some birds maintain a consistent way of life throughout the course of the year, like the brown birds in their Nation of Two. Others have distinct seasonal changes: they might alternate the nesting season's territorial pairs with a winter of solitude (wrens) or of flocking (robins). You need to look at both the breeding and non-breeding seasons to form a full portrait of a bird's attitude toward others.

When you consider these yearly cycles, a fair case can be made that goldfinches are the most consistently agreeable of our neighborhood birds. As with numerous species, they forsake defense of a family territory once nesting is complete, gathering into large flocks that cooperate in finding food and avoiding dangers. Winter goldfinch flocks, along with those of their cousins the linnets, are larger than many in the songbird world, sometimes numbering in the hundreds.

More unusually, goldfinches are also quite tolerant of strangers *during* nesting. Should some pushy neighbor try to visit his partner sitting on the nest, yes, a male may get a little irate. But he declines to let the needs of nesting drive all amiability from his mind. Neighbors are welcome to be neighbors, to build their nests in adjacent trees or even branches, and to join him at the local feeding station. These smaller flocks of spring garner many of the benefits of the larger winter flocks—the quicker awareness of predators and the shared knowledge of food sources. Anyone with a bird feeder can attest to this year-round proclivity for tolerance. Try to find a cozy club of unrelated brown birds, squawkers, wrens, or titmice at your feeders in May. We unobservant giants often class all little birds as benign and harmless creatures, but if you look more closely, you'll find that in springtime most birds are utterly unwelcoming toward strangers of their own species.

Every time a male wren meets another male wren, he feels an irresistible urge to sing, buzz, or chase to drive that aggravating presence from his sight. Goldfinches are relatively unafflicted by that compulsion. In the restrained language of science, we would say that they are a consistently social species. In everyday language, I would say that goldfinches are friendlier than most birds. In spring especially, this can be a bit of a relief: equanimity is less exhausting than the typical avian attitude of implacable prickliness.

Beyond the generally relaxing quality of the goldfinch temperament, such sociability has another consequence familiar to the human experience: it enables abundance. Jays and towhees and other such consistently territorial birds space themselves out and thereby limit their numbers: two here, two down the street, two on the next street over. Like people, goldfinches share the land and its abundant food sources, so that when you walk out your doorway, you cannot help but see your neighbors and hear the thistle-eaters chatter.

For birds with more specialized requirements of food or habitat, tolerance alone wouldn't produce such overall abundance. But the greenbacks' needs are easy to meet throughout most of populated California. Almost any landscape outside of dense forest will comfortably sustain a few dozen finches. Their chief foods are the seeds of thistles and other ubiquitous "weedy" plants. Any tree will hold a little cup nest.

In one particularly wonderful Dawsonism, the great man reacts to the admission of a learned Professor Cooper, author of an *Ornithology of California*, that he "had not met with the nests" of our most abundant goldfinch:

> Not met with them! Shades of Audubon! Where were your eyes? For if there is one virtue which the Green-backed Goldfinch possesses above another, it is that of propagating.

This is a far from negligible benefit of our California goldfinch's relentless amiability: our lives are overflowing with those cheerful, friendly flocks.

Once you become aware of their ubiquity, you will soon start to note the greenbacks' constant conversations, those simpler vocalizations that we describe generally as calls. While the songs of birds are generally the opposite of sociable, being either territorial declarations to warn off other males or invitations in search of a single female auditor, *calls* encompass all the other business that birds have with their peers, from staying in touch to warning of predators. From a purely practical perspective, learning the songs of birds will help you to identify and locate them in spring. But a knowledge of their calls will tell you more, and will do so all year round. To recognize their calls is to understand the language of birds, to know what they are seeing and how they feel about it.

Greenbacks have two calls in particular that I encounter most often. The first is a high, clear whistle, generally considered to have a melancholy tone as it drops in a sinking *tee-yee*. This will often alert you to the presence of perched goldfinches in a treetop and expresses various degrees of uncertainty, from general social status checks to moderate anxiety.

The second greenback sound to know is their flight or contact call, given regularly upon taking off and intermittently in flight, as well as in other situations of close proximity. American goldfinches have a similar, usually four-syllable call, traditionally rendered as "per-chick-o-ree" or "po-ta-to-chip." In greenbacks, it's a series of three to seven short staccato notes with a rather harsh and grating tone, but at a soft and modest volume that can't really hurt your ears. Ralph Hoffman compares the sound to the jarring of cracked glass, while Florence Merriam Bailey terms them "gentle deprecating calls." To realize that those phrases are not an outright contradiction is to develop the subtlety of your hearing.

Wherever I listen around my town, the spring story is much the same: territoriality and aggression fill my ears until I hear those high, sad whistles. A chippie on a treetop repeats his stutter song in stubborn isolation. A jay spreads his wings and squawks in swooping flights along each of his borders. The crows are selective in their tolerance and some sit side by side, but when their loudest ruckus sounds, I look up to see them chasing off a hawk or an unwelcome black-winged stranger.

But from these two treetops come half a dozen sad *tee-yee*s, unaggressively inquiring and responding. And then the greenbacks reach consensus that it's time for an escapade around the block, and all bounce off together murmuring their synchronized tattoo. I hear those signals jarring softly, like pebbles tapping on glass, an even rhythm syncopating with the uneven blinking of their white wings. I watch as the flashing whites dissolve into the distance, then listen as the polysyllables of those pebble taps fade to a fingernail tapping on my mug, to a firm thumb rapping on the table, to the soft flesh of a fingertip gently beating time on the soft flesh of my ear.

The Gold That Never Fades

As I've mentioned, bright plumage is most valuable as a signal of male health among birds that form single-season pair bonds and is less important on average for species with long-term partners. Birds of the finch family belong to the first category and are adorned accordingly, from the all-over magnificence of the goldfinches and linnets to the more selective highlights of siskins and redpolls. When it comes to the goldfinches, however, even Californians sometimes fall into the mistaken belief that our state's second species, the American goldfinch, is the true pinnacle of goldness, the most magnificently yellow, and that this is another area beyond size in which our little western variant rightfully deserves that dismissive appellation of "lesser."

I see how one could make the error. You might look in a field guide and see these two species: the widespread American, extending across the country, bigger and brighter on paper, adjacent to our so-called lesser goldfinch, who is smaller, more restricted in range, and more olive-green and muted. But paper fails to viscerally convey *time*. A male American goldfinch, at his peak, does indeed attain a garish neon that the California greenback forgoes. The former is the pinnacle of goldness for perhaps a four-month window in which he assumes his brilliant summer yellow and his black cap, and even transforms his dull feet and beak to a brighter orange.

But what do the lurid Yankees do as early as July? They start to shed that unnatural and unsustainable brilliance: it's not safe to be that bright, so they retreat into a dull and tired putty. When winter comes, those merely larger Americans will long have lost their glow. The green-backed goldfinches are different and maintain their bright yellow all year round. This is still a vibrant gold, offset in males by a crisp black cap and black wings with bold white patches. So when you stop and stare at the so-called lesser goldfinch's December luminescence, renew your repudiation of that inadequate, specimen-drawer name.

Fortunately, there's no shortage of alternative titles to choose from. South of the border, they are called *jilguero aliblanco* (white-winged goldfinch) or *jilguero capita negra* (black-headed gold-finch). But the chief traditional name that you will find in the older English-language books is "green-backed goldfinch." This is a sturdy appellation that identifies their most distinguishing feature of plumage, whether male or female, at any time of year. And "greenbacks" is easily used in a friendly and convivial way.

Anything is better than "lesser"! Call them California goldfinches to remember your good fortune or Mexican goldfinches if you want to be internationally fair minded—both names have been used. Call them greenbacks if you want to concisely distinguish them from those bigger yellowbacks (that turn to puttybacks in winter). Or simply call them goldfinches, for that gold is in the end their most essential title.

Do we have a more brilliant goldfinch? Only one that fades. Do we have more golden birds? Only furtive natives of the tropics, orioles and tanagers, who spend more time away than here. So when you ask what bird shines brightest in California's amber and green seasons, the answer is this greater goldfinch, who neither forsakes us nor grows gray.

The Little Lyrist and His Song of Many Voices

Male goldfinches sing for the same reason they have bright colors: to impress potential partners. For some birds with more exclusionary instincts, like the brown chippies or mockingbirds, the declaration of a territory to rival males can be another important use of song, but the clues all suggest that females of their own species are the greenbacks' primary audience: they are not highly territorial overall, their songs are excessively complex for mere territorial delineation, and they often sing directly in front of a female auditor, either from a perch or in a targeted display flight.

In truth, when the scientists speak of this bird, they don't debate green backs, white wings, or size. They call him *Spinus psaltria*, the lyre-playing finch. Music is his greatest talent.

So many times I've walked out from a doorway, from my home or from a shop, and in these paved-over places heard that music flowing out. Those high and lissom voices ramble on and on, skipping weightlessly out into the air of these unwild settings. They seem to dance across a hundred whistles and squeaks, buzzes and rattles, and never pause for breath, but from time to time I hear an interjected high *tee-yee* to remind me of the author of that wild panoply of sound. The greenbacks sing in many places and they sing in many months, but I never grow tired of listening, for they also sing in many voices.

Each bird might have a repertoire of up to a hundred or so unique phrases. About 10 percent of a typical song consists of the call notes I introduced earlier: listen for those staccato flight calls as introduction and then interspersed, sinking *tee-yee*s. Another 40 percent is made up of assorted notes used only within songs. The remaining 50 percent are imitated calls or song fragments from other birds. All three of these components demonstrate goldfinches' insatiable musical appetite, their hunger for new sounds.

I described the greenback's familiar contact call as a series of "short staccato notes." But our clumsy human ears only hear the surface. Across all the members of the finch family for which this question has to my knowledge been asked, it appears that those staccato flight calls are used for *individual* recognition. They sound the same to us, but in reality the males subtly change their flight calls to match those of their female partners, so that each pair of birds shares a unique and private password, which they utter to keep in touch as well as in more intimate conversation. Goldfinches learn from their mates.

The next 40 percent of their songs, the nonimitative song

components, are also not mere random chatter. Within a given area, goldfinches will share many of these notes, while having a different repertoire than birds in other regions: these phrases are not a genetic heritage that simply popped into their beaks, but pieces of music that they learned from hearing other males sing. Without their yearly flocking conferences, their songs would be impoverished. Goldfinches learn from their peers.

The remaining 50 percent is the most interesting of all: their imitations of other birds. Greenbacks love to copy short sounds they've heard and scatter them pell-mell throughout their songs, often drawing on a total of some thirty to forty different species. In our California neighborhoods, only the mockingbird challenges the greenback as a mimic, but even mockers can't keep up, can't pour as many memories into a minute's music.

Goldfinches are the virtuosos, their mimicry rushing out in an impatient cascade—a twenty-second song might reproduce a dozen different sources. I aspire to a perfect familiarity with the calls of all my local birds, and this is the constant test that shows me how far I am from fluency: I listen to the greenback songs and try to hear the birds they've heard.

The story grows deeper when we realize that goldfinches imitate birds that aren't present on their nesting grounds. They aren't simply repeating the sounds they hear around them at the time (a plausible layman's hypothesis) or that they heard during the first few months of their lives (a plausible scientist's hypothesis, since many other birds have an initial period of song learning, after which their repertoire is fixed). Instead, they continue to add to their repertoires for at least several months and quite likely throughout the few years of their lives, remembering sounds they hear in their days of winter roaming.

Remember this when you hear the greenbacks sing: their lack of territoriality makes the musician's education possible. Their songs are not inborn and instinctive, nor limited to the neighbors they were born with, as with the mockingbird who stays at home. Goldfinches travel, are exposed to new friends and alien creatures, and then retain those memories and stitch them into songs.

Like people telling stories of past adventures to impress their listeners with the breadth of their experience, the greenbacks sing the unfamiliar voices of their California wandering. A bird might nest in the woodland and introduce calls from the chaparral among the bays and buckeyes. He might nest in the suburbs and recall sounds from the farm fields. He sings the notes of finches he has met and creatures his courted listener has never heard, reproducing all with a fidelity that no human storyteller can match.

Who crosses the borders? Who has heard what lies beyond? The little lyrist is the tale teller who has voyaged and come home. In his garrulous excitement, he sings from the treetops and he sings from the sky. A hundred sounds breathlessly come forth, bird after bird instantly alive: flicker and flycatcher, robin, swallow, kestrel.

The Greenbacks Fly beside Me

I can find them any day, those friendly, golden singers who, like me, never cease to listen. On my way to work, I ride along the path that goes between the hospital and train tracks. The habitat is no native paradise, dominated as it is by chain link and great clumps of blackberry and fennel. But between those marks of human presence flies a string of yellow birds, dipping and alive.

Their white wings flash, and their backs of black-rubbed green merge into the landscape as they take off before me. But when they see I pose no threat, the greenbacks abandon their escape, reverse course, and reveal their fronts of gold. Those gentle deprecating calls connect the pairs in reassurance like a clasp of hands, and reassure me also that there is nothing to disturb their peace:

neither I nor any other has provoked their sense of danger. I hear the same music of birds at ease outside my springtime windows, where a host of yellow singers tell gently competing tales of their now completed journeys.

No bird outshines these living flowers that rise and fly up from the grasses, leaving their less brilliant rivals anchored to the ground. No bird outsings the little lyrists who each year travel and tell in pride of what they've heard. But what makes these glories sweeter are their gentle authors all around me: birds who shine without the fear of all the greater goldens and sing without the anger of those whose songs are walls.

CHAPTER 8
DEVOTION'S FRUIT

Mourning Dove, *Zenaida macroura*

Dove raced Falcon and Hummingbird through California's valleys long before the foreign names and strange straight lines were inscribed on the maps. Many have heard their mournful cries and wondered whom they longed for. And when you see two doves perching side by side throughout the summer, then you see an ancient image of those who dissolve their separation and find completion in each other.

For most people, in most times and in most places, birds were enmeshed within our lives, made relevant by folktales, religion, and everyday common knowledge. Due to the disruptive course of human history on this continent, we often now find ourselves lacking such connections with the birds around us; if there were old stories of the brown birds and the greenbacks, they have been scattered and now are hard to find. But for other birds, the old meanings have not quite disappeared and are ready still to guide you. Of few is this more true than the mourning dove.

Stories change mere knowledge into meaning. You won't need to scramble after disparate facts once you find these anchors to doves as characters and actors. You won't need to ask what bird that is, disappearing through the trees or singing sadly in the distance. You will know who flies the fastest and why the mourner cries.

The Swift

I love to watch birds flying on the most blustery of days. I'll watch as a bluebird or a kestrel beats up into a deafening wind with enormous effort, waiting for the moment when she decides to change course, when she tucks and turns and dares the wind to throw her with all the speed that it can muster. Sometimes I miss the prologue, my body hunched and head bowed as I trudge into the air's resistance until some winged form blazes by and disappears on the periphery of my vision. On days like this, it's hard to hear and hard to look ahead: birds drop like falling stars, unexpected and ungraspable.

Mourning doves can give this impression when there is no wind at all. Whether I'm daydreaming or alert doesn't make much difference—I'll be walking along in a quite clearly doveless setting when a streamlined gray-brown bullet of a bird whips into view and out of it. Sometimes I'll hear a distinctive whistling of wings, not so much an advance warning as a notice of departure, the sound already fading to silence as my bewildered eyes finally catch up to see the disappearing bird.

This is not most people's image when they think of doves. Most people probably think of them as we see them more often, not on the wing, but perched or walking with their clumsy, waddling step. When not in flight, mourning doves appear ungainly, with legs too short for their large bodies. At a glance, they appear not so much vigorous as vulnerable. Their eyes are ringed in pale blue and set within a tiny head, giving them a perpetual expression of wide-eyed innocence or ingenuous astonishment. Speed, power, or even effectiveness can seem antithetical to their character.

But the figure that you see tiptoeing with difficulty along a slender branch does not reflect the dove's full nature. To see a mourning dove more fully means you must also see those moments when she casts aside her clumsiness and when her short legs become as unimportant as those of hummingbirds and swallows. Walking doves are fish momentarily out of water; when they take to the sky, they enter in their element. Doves take flight, and other birds then seem the slow and awkward ones. Crows and jays, finches and sparrows—none of these come close to keeping up.

Of course, this is no biological accident. As is true for many birds, rapid flight is one of the most important countermeasures against predators. If you are relatively large and less nimble at quick changes of direction, then a short scurry under branches is not the flight you need: absolute acceleration, an immediate distancing from danger is the mourning dove's first recourse. Efficiency on the wing is also invaluable for a wide-ranging life in general. Some mourning dove populations undertake long latitudinal migrations, and even those that don't are far from sedentary, with an often expansive daily range between roosting, feeding, and watering areas. Fast flight creates safety by stretching time and creates opportunity by diminishing distance.

It's easy to forget all this and think of doves as clumsy trundlers. Beginners at watching birds often see a fleeting form departing and exclaim "Hawk!" or "Falcon!" in excitement. For some reason they are disappointed to learn that it was a mourning dove. They needn't be. The speed that they admire is the same. The dove is the falcon's equal.

The dove is the falcon's equal. This is the oldest race in California, and neither bird yet admits defeat. The most frequently recurring trait of doves in the stories of Native Californians is speed.

One Miwok tale tells of Falcon's journey to the end of the world in search of his dead father. To reach him, he must leap through a constantly opening and closing hole in the sky. This is not easy. Falcon's wife, Duck, makes the attempt and fails. He tests the portal with an arrow—the passage snaps shut and the arrow is broken. Falcon thinks that only he can make the jump, but he is mistaken: Dove can also make it through. In another Miwok story, Falcon again thinks he can outrace Dove and again is proven wrong: "We run the same. We run the same. I did not think that you could run so fast." Hummingbird, the third of California's legendary speedsters, issues the same challenge to Dove and meets the same result: "When he and I race, it is a tie . . . he and I will travel together for all time."

Doves are the devourers of distance and honored for this role. Among the Yokuts and Western Mono in south-central California, inherited totemic associations determined key tribal positions: eagles or falcons were the totems of chieftain lines, while birds such as ravens or magpies might be associated with other community roles. These were vividly lived relationships: one would venerate, speak to, and dream of his totemic animal, and never kill or eat its living exemplars. According to A. H. Gayton's survey of some forty different tribes in this region, the only invariable among these animal associations was that of doves with the position of the *winatum*, the Yokuts term sometimes translated as "messenger," but actually encompassing numerous prestigious responsibilities involving communication between tribes, communication between chiefs and their people, and important ceremonial functions.

Honor the winatum, the one who goes between. Like doves, they cross all borders: distance and rank are no impediments, and even strange portals to worlds beyond our own open to their passage. Admire the racer that does not fall behind either the falcon or the hummingbird, but matches them beat for beat to the ending of the earth and the ending of all time.

When a dove disappears rapidly from my sight, I never find myself regretting that she didn't linger longer, nor wish that she had been instead some fiercer bird of prey. Why would I? I love it when I lift my head at the sound of whistling wings and catch a momentary glimpse of a bird just risen above the treetops, suspended for a single second like an arrow set to the string. In that second is a space to relish what I know is coming next. In that second, I remember that Dove flies more quickly than Falcon's fastest arrow. One heartbeat sounds—then she slides into her private tempest, and like the wind she's gone.

The Yearning

I often see doves disappearing; often I don't see them at all. The second story told of doves is not one that we see, but rather one we hear. "Zenaida is a vesper bird," one old-time ornithologist summed up. What he had in mind was not a vision, but a sound, the slow and melancholy cooing that gives mourning doves their name.

Specifically, he was referring to the mourning dove's habit of singing in the late afternoon and evening. Some birds sing most notably at dawn, but the ideal time for listening to mourning doves is in the closing stages of a warm spring day, when the memory of cooler months is still fresh enough to imbue mere lounging in the sun with positive pleasure.

I can think of many such afternoons in my years of peak Thoreauvianism, when I lived a blessedly car- and internet-free existence within the ample two hundred square feet of a yurt on the edge of a Bay Area woodland. I would hear violet-green swallows singing in the predawn darkness overhead and a glorious triumphant chorus with the rising of the sun. Later, as the day drew to its close, I might enjoy a few hours of hammocked idleness, with occasional glances at a book, rather more gazing at the sky, and a high likelihood of pleasant drowsiness. That's when the mourning dove song took center stage, when the lively and combative songs had faded away and the bees were droning in the warm air.

I am undecided whether robins, meadowlarks, or California quail make for the best alarm clock. But for a lullaby I have no hesitation: rock me in the mourning dove's soft and steady murmur.

coo-AAAHH-coo . . . coo . . . coo . . . coo . . .

A first note expands and slurs upward to a higher pitch, then deflates into two to four more cooing notes that trail off in melancholy indeterminacy. Doves in general share very soft and gentle voices, but mourning doves are the softest of the soft when it comes to tenderness of tone, languorously stretching out their songs with slurs and silences. Why does this song strike so many as mournful? The answer is straightforward to musicians: the mourning dove song begins with a consistent interval, a rising minor third. The third is the crucial note that determines whether we are in a major or minor key, a "happy" or "sad" one in the standard simplification.

This is a magic interval. I obsessed over it for years when I was younger. I played the cello and would endlessly repeat the opening of Bach's D-minor cello suite, which begins with the mourning dove interval. I played the erhu, the higher-pitched Chinese bowed instrument, and endlessly repeated Liu Tianhua's "Meditation on a Single String," which begins with the mourning dove interval. The Chinese version went one better, removing the fingerboard and encouraging audible sliding between notes to add a mourning dove *slur*. Take any song of loss, sorrow, pain, or longing: this is the interval that makes it that way. This is the interval that the mourning dove sings.

That sense of loss and sorrow is the most immediately apparent of the narratives we've attached to mourning doves, embedded as it is within their name. I do not think there is any bird on the continent that is more widely recognized by ear with such specificity: people might hear a crow or owl and apply those generic terms, but very few of the official two-part names have penetrated popular consciousness in the way that "mourning dove" has. This is because the name was not decreed from on high but canonized in its traditional form. If all our bird names were based on what real people hear and see, then more people would know the names of birds, as they do with this one.

The fundamental musical pathos of the mourning dove's song has then been fitted into a few different narrative elaborations. The specifically mourning context in fact predates our English name, suggesting the universality I claim: a Yurok story from far northern California describes the origin of this sound in a story of the dove lamenting a lost grandfather. Many modern writers blend the sadness with traditional motifs of dove romanticism from western culture and describe longing, yearning, or incompleteness. "Their plaintive call suggests irresistibly a kind of seeking-out, the attempt by separated souls to restore a lost communion," wrote Edward Abbey.

The underlying physics of an affecting musical interval constitutes a real form of truth, even if it doesn't form a full portrait of what's in the singer's mind. A world that's full of music is a rich one, and when plaintive songs of minor thirds float out from the trees, it is natural that they attract our attention. There are dove stories built on this which help that song stand out, and it can do the same to realize that the doves are singing an even older and more universal theme, one built on the magic ratios that create harmony in the wild world of sound.

Lower pitched than other daylight birds, the dove mourns in

a cello's voice. But his instrument has shed the friction of bows that scrape on strings, and his music has left virtuosity behind to perfect a simple tune. He slides with flawless smoothness from one note to a higher, and then back down again. Over and over, the doves lift me and they lower me through the days of spring and summer. They rock me with a longing song in the days of warmth and sunlight.

The Completed

How does that minor chord resolve?

Two mourning doves sit quietly together on a roofline, wings touching. The male with his gray-blue cap stretches his beak toward his partner, gently inserting it in hers as if to feed a nestling. The two pump their necks together with their whole bodies in the motion. They separate, and he half lifts his wings—they are lined in hidden blue. She reaches her own beak into that softness, like one who slips a hand inside another's coat to feel the warmth within the wool rise and fall with the wearer's breath. As he folds his wings, her beak moves upward, traces his back, finds the sheen on his nape and scratches, back and forth. The rosy iridescence glimmers as she ruffles through those feathers and his eyes shut in his pleasure.

Here is another true story. Doves are ancient symbols of romantic devotion:

> My dove in the clefts of the rock . . .
>
> Let me hear your voice,
>
> your delicious song.
>
> I love to look at you.

The most sensual book of the Hebrew Bible, the Song of Songs, returns repeatedly to doves for its central metaphors of mutual adoration both audible and visible. Some two thousand years later, Victor Hugo had one of his characters sum up essentially the same trait of doves as an encapsulation of a romantic philosophy: "Adore each other. . . . The only sages in creation are the turtle doves. The philosophers say to moderate your joys. I say to give them full rein." The idea is ubiquitously embedded in western culture between and since these examples: see the release of doves at weddings, Christmas songs about the appropriate number of turtledoves to receive from one's true love (two, of course), and the phrase *lovey-dovey* to describe hopelessly unabashed expressions of affection.

It's true of other doves of the world, and it's true of ours: mated mourning doves adore each other. Start with the song, the male's expression of how he feels *before* he finds his partner. It's true that there is no clear biological division between the confident song of the robin and the melancholy song of the mourning dove. But I think it's appropriate to remember that birdsong's invitation is prompted by an overwhelming sense of dissatisfaction. Doves coo constantly to announce that an unpaired male is holding a territory. After finding a mate, cooing typically decreases by more than 90 percent. Our sense of yearning incompleteness is not wrong: this is a song the lonely sing.

First, male doves sing and fight off rivals in their territory. Once a mate is found, the tenderness expands in scenes like the one described earlier, full of mate feeding and allopreening, as scientists term these behaviors. More simply, he makes her dinner, and they exchange caresses. Song is largely replaced by shorter "nest calls," which seem analogous to what is called "quiet song" in some species—an intimate communication between mated birds that is a bonding ritual in itself rather than strictly limited to practical purposes. Nest construction is the most charmingly congenial of all: the male gathers twigs, flies to the nest site, and presents them to his partner for her judicious placement. Sometimes he'll stand on her back to make the handoff. Doves presumably do these things because to do them feels delightful.

Why are doves more visibly enthusiastic about their mates than most birds? The evolutionary purpose of these behaviors is to reinforce the pair bond. For many birds, such maintenance activities aren't worth it: the bonds between most songbird couples fade away after a few months. (This book contains a disproportionate number of long-term monogamous species because they are interesting.) Mourning dove nesting season, by contrast, is notable for both its duration and intensity: up to six months long, raising up to six broods of young. Each brood of two is raised as quickly as possible. A primary ingredient in this strategy is an unusually large contribution from the male, who performs a significant share of incubation and a majority of parenting, taking over feeding of the fledglings while the female begins the next cycle. Biologist Bernd Heinrich sums up the evolutionary coherence of the process:

> Their minimal nest; covering of eggs, young, and feces; freezing of all motion; absence of any begging vocalizations of the chicks; very fast growth; and staying in the nest until expert flight was possible—all point to predator avoidance as a unifying strategy. Predator avoidance may also explain the structure of the nest, the number of eggs, and the crop feeding, as well as the obsessive nest sitting. This strategy requires the presence of the male to provision the sitting female and to relieve her at the nest. Without a partner, it would not be possible.

There is a secret to mourning doves' success, an essential current running through their entire playbook: cooperation between the pair, sustained by constant bond-reinforcing activities. We may read old stories of doves' devotion and suspect they are mere sentimental dressing. But all that tender nibbling has a distinct biological function leading to distinct evolutionary success. The average life span of a mourning dove is only a year, yet there are four hundred million mourning doves. They are one of the contenders for most numerous bird on the continent. The evidence of doves' devotion is based not on poems, novels, or traditions but on this solid fact: from eggs to independents, six broods in a year. The firmest proof of those ties' strength is the landscape filled with doves.

What Lingers in the Air

Like their falcon-matching speed, fecundity is a response to frailty—one that triumphs. Signs of mildness and affection, as with the doves' soft and lonely songs or their tendency to flight, mislead us into thinking that this bird is weaker than it is. The aggression of the crows and jays or the finches' quick return to the safety of the flock are not the only ways to thrive.

I come around a bend and spot a mourning dove, gray-brown and spotted like the ground. She's seen me first: her head perks up to betray alarm through the constant blue-ringed wideness of her eyes. And even though I attempt my most unalarming passage, she bursts from the woods and vanishes, leaving only empty air.

But in that still and quiet space after the wave and whistle of her departure, I hear distant voices rise and fall in their slow slide along the string. A single dove soon disappears, but the mourning doves will not soon vanish. When I am old, I may not hear the waxwings' whispers, and the dawn chorus may grow quieter. But in this bird I place my faith down to my final spring.

Flight is not a sign of weakness: it is their strongest fortress. Those birds are crying out their loneliness, because they aim to end it. And each spring I will hear doves again, the fruit of their devotion.

CHAPTER 9
THE DUSKY DEMON

Northern Mockingbird, *Mimus polyglottos*

This celebrated and very extraordinary bird, in extent and variety of vocal powers, stands unrivalled by the whole feathered songsters of this or perhaps any other country; and shall receive from us, in this place, all that attention and respect which superior merit is justly entitled to.

—Alexander Wilson, *American Ornithology*, 1828

I have been cataloguing the particular excellencies of several prominent singing birds: robins, finches, doves. Each has its own unique and superlative quality. But the mockingbird's song isn't remarkable from one singular perspective but from every point of view. The competitive eagerness of robins who can hardly wait for day, the virtuosity of goldfinches who speak with thirty voices, and the doves' audible evolution from loneliness to deep devotion—all are mustered on parade by the king of song.

He doesn't claim preeminence in size, or strength, or color. In the quiet intervals of the year, he is discreet—it's not hard to find people who don't recognize him by sight, who think they've never seen him. But inside that slim gray form is a singer that commands attention. Robin sings at dawn, but the mockingbird sings while robins sleep. Linnets seem lighthearted; mockers seem obsessed. A goldfinch shares his thirty voices proudly; a mockingbird knows a hundred. Doves mourn until they find their partner, and then they find relief. The dusky demon never does.

The trivia that make up the mockingbird's nonmusical life are quick to summarize. Mockingbirds are a familiar sight in most neighborhoods: gray and white, jay-size birds who patrol lawns for insects and forage in shrubs for berries. Their plumage appears nondescript, except when they fly or perform courtship dances that reveal the white patches in their wings and outer tail feathers.

Mockingbirds are found across the country and extend well beyond our national borders into South America. Here in California, they are largely nonmigratory: both mated pairs and bachelor males maintain year-round territories. Historically, mockers are native to southern California deserts and chaparral, but their range has expanded northward over the last hundred years in lockstep with expanding human habitation, which creates their ideal assemblage of open areas, fruiting trees, and abundant perches and platforms to sing from. Today we have them wherever we've made such changes, from orchards to the suburbs, up and down the state. There are birds we have displaced or lost in our insatiable colonization, but we have this consolation: the mockingbirds advance beside us and make our home their own.

And that's about all you need to know regarding Beethoven's preferred breakfast and commute habits. Because there really is only one overriding topic here, whether considered for its indelible impression on human listeners or for its prominence in the birds' own lives: those unending songs of countless flowing voices.

Our Own Music, Varied, Powerful, and Free

No birdsong has been more celebrated within the American tradition. Wilson's praise is typical of a century's worth of avian patriotism championing our native singer, who was dubbed by Audubon "the king of song" above the Old World's nightingales and skylarks. The poets took up the cause, none more so than Walt Whitman, who found in the mockingbird a fitting representative for his American poetic mission. Listen, he said, to the mockingbird's chants, that voice "that can make the vaults of America ring . . . sing it with varied and powerful idioms . . . our own song, free, joyous, and masterful."

If we don't usually state our pride in such bald terms today, it's because we now take that nineteenth-century contention for granted. Few of us would think to place our nation's natural splendors behind those of England or Germany. In California least of all: we are the state of redwoods and bigtrees, oceans and mountains. And when we enumerate our country's broader points of pride, we should not overlook this one, small and gray and familiar though he is: the mockingbird is native here and takes a fitting place beside the condor.

What did Audubon and Wilson hear when they listened to this song? Let's begin with the basics, as a human hears them. Mockingbird song is made up of long series of repeated phrases, which may be ideas of the bird's own invention, imitations of other birds, or imitations of human-originating sounds. They will typically repeat a given motif several times, then another, and another, and so on, sometimes singing for over an hour at a stretch. People often ask me how they can tell a mockingbird apart from what he's imitating, but it really isn't difficult. When I go for a walk in a marsh-side neighborhood in my town and hear a song of three repeated pretty whistles, then five "unlockings of the car," and then four squeaky *ki-ki-doo*s of the black rail, I am unlikely to think that I am listening to either a Honda or an elusive marsh bird. The exact sequence may be completely novel to me, but the fact that it is a sequence of repeated, disparate sounds tells me exactly who the singer is.

The unique and most frequently praised aspect of mockingbird song is obviously this imitative extravagance, which seems to be nearly unlimited by any question of technical feasibility. In wild settings, the calls of other birds are dominant motifs. Nowadays, suburban mockers compose medleys of neighborhood birds, car alarms, and cell phones. Everything is reproduced with perfect fidelity in a constantly developing repertoire of hundreds of sounds. *Sinsonte* is the mockingbird's name in much of Central America, from an ancient Náhuatl name meaning "four-hundred-voices." That tally is not far off.

The mockingbird's song is ubiquitous in our experience—they live where people do, and sing for many months of the year and for many hours of the day. They sing with a sheer overpowering volume that is hard to miss, especially at night when other birds fall silent. Combine this inability to be overlooked with their genius for mimicry, and you can easily understand how both our naturalists and poets were drawn to praise this bird.

But our few hundred years of modern acclaim merely continue an ancient continental story. Not for centuries but for millennia, humans have recognized this bird's undampened trumpet of a voice and inexhaustible invention. You and I can hear it too, right outside our doors.

I walk down the daylit street and hear it ring above the cars and motors. I step out in the moonlight and hear it flowing onward when we have grown weary and retire. And in that ever-changing song I hear my neighborhood repeated and transformed. I hear the poet's bird take the mundane words of others and turn them into music, take in our New World's voices and weave them into song.

Somewhere Listening Must Be the One I Want

Spring is the season of song and nesting because those two activities are intimately tied together. It's easy to elide the birds' motivations into some simplified narrative of either longing or delighted exuberance, but we've seen how musical intentions can vary significantly among birds, from the simple territorial insistence of the towhees to the ornate competitions of goldfinches. Mourning doves begin with a basic territorial announcement, but even when paired, periodically resume cooing between broods and liberally engage in quieter "nest coos" as part of their broader bond-maintenance rituals. Mockingbirds employ their music for all of those underlying functions: territoriality, courtship, and pair maintenance. The result is a song that is remarkable in several parallel dimensions: for its indefatigable performance, its musical complexity, and its extended continuance into summer.

Those past sentiments of human admiration touched on these results that we can hear, even when we only saw their underlying causes in broad and general outline. But the more closely we trace each strand in this song's evolution, the richer and more intricate grows our appreciation of the tapestry.

Territorial Night-Singing Favors Volume over Variety

A first clue to the primary function of a song: is it complex and variable, or simple and stereotyped? Elaborate songs like those of the goldfinches form a good basis for comparison between males: we assume that the complexity developed to make the song more useful for females' assessment of potential mates. Simple songs like the nearly identical trills practiced by the brown chippies are less informative about the singer's fitness and seem to be given primarily to indicate one's territory to other males. Do mockingbirds fall neatly to one side or the other on this scale?

In practice, they seem to sing in both styles. Mockingbirds have famously elaborate songs that clearly developed in response to female choosiness, and they sing their most complex and varied songs when courting a specific female. But they are also extremely territorial, and practice what is almost a separate song to warn off rival males. These territorial songs are much less varied—by mockingbird standards—and possess another unique quality suggestive of this different purpose: they continue into the night.

This is probably the second most remarked-on trait of mockingbird song, after the imitative exuberance. Essentially none of our other songbirds sing nocturnally. The middle of the night is not when the females are conducting their evaluations of prospective partners. They are, sensibly, sleeping.

By the standards of any other bird, these would still be remarkable songs. The basic pattern is the same, but the diversity and imitative content is greatly reduced: one study noted that if the authors were to have estimated a subject mockingbird's repertoire based on his night songs, they would have produced an estimate of 82 song elements, but if based on his daytime courtship songs, they would have calculated a total of 209.

At night, mockingbirds hold back their energy from creative invention and feats of memory, instead throwing everything they have into volume and vigor. They play to their audience, and this is not an audience that respects nuance. This is an audience that respects force, power, and presence. These blunt songs of low diversity and high intensity exist to tell neighboring males that there is an unsleeping defender present, tireless and alert.

Females receive the lengthy serenades adorned with diverse and striking quotations. Males are greeted by a battle chant, unrelentingly repeated.

The Virtuosity of Courtship

Of course, it is the unending inventiveness of the mockingbird's courtship songs that has received the most human attention and admiration. These songs are analogous to the elaborate singing of the greenbacks and the like: the more complex a song is, the more strongly it indicates an individual's mental and physical health, suggesting that he is a well-nourished and capable forager, unhampered by any grave genetic defects, and therefore a solid candidate for fatherhood. This signaling is accurate: birds with the most complex songs successfully raise more young than birds with less impressive repertoires.

A good chunk of mockingbird singing is accompanied by a sort of dance, a series of skyward leaps that show off their white wing patches. Playful chases of the courted female and constant chases of intruders demonstrate speed and agility. Mockingbirds also have the charming habit of leading tours of their territory to newly arrived females, with special attention given to prospective nest sites. Males will follow up these tours with actual construction, often framing two or three nests for female approval and subsequent furnishing with a softer lining.

These are all expressions of courtship, exertions made by a male when a female appears within his little kingdom. This moment of arrival is when the scientists record the maximal feats of song, those repertoires of hundreds of distinct phrases. Mockingbirds are not adorned with brilliant plumage. Appearances count for little next to effort and intelligence. A rich territory gets you in the door, athleticism never hurts, and nest building shows diligence. But there is no greater proof of worth than those songs to which he dedicates his hours. If a mockingbird could tell you how he intends to set himself apart, his answer would be this:

Sing a song for weeks, for her ears alone. Play a hundred parts, with unending novel voices. And when your rivals' melodies trail off and their repertoires run short, then she will know the difference between the king of song and mere pretenders.

The Courtship Does Not End: Song as Bond Reinforcement

Mockingbirds thus perform territorial bachelor songs with unmatched persistence, and courtship songs with unmatched variety. But they are also monogamous birds with long-term bonds. So what explains the continuing flood of song from the many males in *established* pairs?

Studies have found that mockingbirds, as with certain other species, use song as a tool for mate synchronization: when the female hears her partner singing, a hormonal response is triggered that prepares her for the next nesting cycle. This practical function is more valuable in species such as mockingbirds that nest several times each year. (Three broods are common in California; up to six are seen in Florida.) He begins to sing; she prepares to lay eggs.

But the resumption of song can also be legitimately seen as an act of resumed courtship, as a way of asserting primacy over never fully vanquished rivals. Song ceases during incubation and nestling feeding: this is the time for secrecy from predators, as well as the period when female fidelity can be most counted on. (Newly launched adultery is rare with babies in the cradle.) But then the young fledge, and that's the dangerous moment for the insecure husband. There are known cases of mockingbird "sequential polyandry," in which the female mates with an available neighbor once her fledged young are old enough to be cared for by their father alone. So that is when he works and sings, in order that she won't forget all his good qualities.

What's going on, in short, is *ongoing* assessment by the female.

Female choice is not limited in mockingbirds to the initial court-ship period, is not confined to a brief window in which her decision is made and her fate is set. Mockingbirds favor long-term monog-amy, but they do so with the ever-present possibilities of both adultery and divorce. Even well-established mocker pairs can split up. They may have nested together in the past, even successfully raised young together, but if the nests begin to fail—suggestive of his inadequacy as provisioner, defender, or genetic contributor—or someone better moves in next door, she will leave.

That possibility is what drives the male mockingbird's ongoing fervor to impress. And it's not just the singing, which could be put down to mere synchronizing of the biological watches as described earlier. The overall distribution of the conjugal workload indicates a tilt toward female advantage in this species: male parental invest-ment is higher than that of females and distinctly higher than the average among male songbirds. They have to work.

Males perform the majority of nest construction, a substantial task given the five or so nests they will often build each season (a new one for each clutch, plus a few unused proposal nests). Males undertake most of the dangerous defensive duties, an activity in which they are famously aggressive, whether facing off with other mockers, potential predators, or even such outsized intruders as nest-disrupting humans. Very few two-ounce songbirds want to pick a fight with us. But the reality is that female mockingbirds pre-fer aggressive males, so the dragons must be faced. Most unusu-ally, males take on the majority of the child feeding, assuming essentially all parental responsibility for the latter two of the three weeks during which fledglings are dependent.

This is extremely atypical among American songbirds. In the majority of cases, males take a lesser or equal share in nest building and child feeding and then hurry back to carefree bachelorhood. A minority of species pair up and stick together until death does them part. Doves achieve a similar level of labor distribution, but the mechanisms of male motivation seem to be much more carrot and less stick, built on reciprocal demonstrations of affection that are comparatively invisible in mockingbirds. Very few birds are so strongly faced with the mocker's stern taskmaster of Ongoing Female Assessment. And so it is that very few birds sing like this one.

He met her before his first birthday. He lived for six years more and kept her always by his side. He chased the rivals on his borders and fought the threats against his family. He built her thirty nests and fed their fifty children, so she would have no cause to leave.

But the ever-present ritual of a six-year mocker marriage? That he sang to her in March, in June, and in August just the same. Each time he sang, he added new instruments to the orchestra inside him, seeking something new to charm her. So when summer wanes and birds grow quiet, as one by one the sunrise voices fade, you will still hear song's sovereign, crown intact and head unbowed. He lifts his song again for that one who listens still.

Our Dusky Demon and Brother

It is very hard for us to say with confidence what exactly a singing bird feels. Sometimes we can rule out our clumsiest suppositions when we consider the context in which a bird sings: a bachelor's song of territorial aggression, for instance, should not be characterized as one of the giddily lovesick. Making definite statements is harder, but I think that we should still try to make them, with some caveats in place, to avoid the equally erroneous implication of entirely unemotional language—birds certainly feel *something* when they sing.

A lonely night-singing mockingbird is not fulfilling a function in mere robotic automatism. You don't sing the blues through long sleepless nights because it feels like the simple, easy course. You don't become the king of song through blithe freedom from cares. To exclude all sympathy from our interpretation would be an intellectual mistake, would undoubtedly omit a crucial chapter of the story.

Science rightfully corrects our misunderstandings. But within the bounds of science there is still space for feelings, for elemental emotions we can relate to. From the other side, poems and narratives can render the situations and reactions that we legitimately share with animals with more affecting directness than possible in minutely verifiable studies. That's why the best rendition of the mockingbird's song that I know is found in Walt Whitman's "Out of the Cradle Endlessly Rocking," in which the poet tells the story of a mockingbird's loss of his mate and subsequent grief. Whitman is attentive to ornithological detail—of the nest and eggs, the migration pattern, the cadence and timing of the song—but the most important thing he captures that more restrained renditions don't is depth of feeling, a sense of compulsion and irresolvable dissatisfaction:

Land! Land! O land!

Whichever way I turn, O I think you could give me my mate back again if you only would,

For I am almost sure I see her dimly whichever way I look.

O rising stars!

Perhaps the one I want so much will rise, will rise with some of you.

O throat! O trembling throat!

Sound clearer through the atmosphere!

Pierce the woods, the earth,

Somewhere listening to catch you must be the one I want.

Whitman's repetitions and short vocative phrases are deliberate re-creations of mockingbird song; the style reveals the intent. One could quibble over the dividing line between a lament of remembering a lost mate and the longing of other bachelor mockingbirds likewise singing in nocturnal loneliness, but such quibbling risks eclipsing the fundamental truth of Whitman's transcription: somewhere listening must be the one I want.

The poet describes his task as "translating . . . the song of his dusky demon and brother." That is what I try to do, and what anyone listening closely to birds should attempt. Keep those sibling songs with you and chant them again. Render them into words you can understand, knowing that translation requires honesty and knowledge, but also imagination, a dash of invention to bridge the gap between two languages of imperfect alignment.

Why can't he sleep, the dusky demon in the moonlight? Why does he strut and parade his four hundred mercury rhymes? And why does he keep singing, though he has lived with her a lifetime? Because there are other lonely voices in the night, and he must not yield the stage. Because now that he has found her, he must tell her every word he knows. And because he is haunted by a fear that never goes away, the fear of life without her should his music ever falter.

CHAPTER 10
AUTUMN KINGS

White-crowned Sparrow, *Zonotrichia leucophrys*
Golden-crowned Sparrow, *Zonotrichia atricapilla*

Fall comes, and days grow shorter. The black oak leaves turn yellow, and the birds no longer sing. September fades into October, and even the most fervent of musicians, mockingbirds and goldfinches, give only rare and intermittent bursts of melody. But then one morning a clear, high fluting rings out, three sweet whistles in a dying fall. The crowned sparrows have returned.

There are two of them, the golden-crowned and the white-crowned sparrow, and both have songs characterized by those distinct high whistles, notes that are unusually clear and single pitched, and so more like human music than most birdsong. In the golden-crowned sparrow, the typical California pattern consists of three descending notes ("Oh dear me" or "I'm so tired"), though you will often hear only two, or an alternate pattern that descends to the second note before rising to the third. In white-crowned sparrows, a basic theme runs through numerous variations: a single clear introductory whistle, followed by a jumble of buzzes and trills.

Soon enough we'll see them, these two large sparrows that feed in ubiquitous flocks in parks and weedy fields, on the edges of paths and dusty roads. The basics of crowned sparrow identification are simple: if a sparrow has a golden crown, it's a golden-crowned sparrow, and if a sparrow has head stripes of crisp black and white, it's a white-crowned sparrow. Both species like to have some nearby cover to retreat to should any danger threaten, but often hop out into exposed areas as they search for fallen seeds, a smattering of insects, and the fresh new plant growth that soon arrives with the winter rains.

What are sparrows? The popular prejudice is that they are a group of indistinguishable little brown birds. More accurately, we could note that they are a family of modestly sized songbirds adapted to eating seeds and feeding on the ground, whose members are often migratory, social in winter, and musical in spring. All these traits have their exceptions within the large family, but all are applicable to the two crowned sparrows. Overall, they are fitting representatives of the larger tribe, with their greatest exceptionality being their vibrant repudiation of that dismissive "indistinguishable." After all, they wear crowns, the right word for the colors on their high-held and singing heads.

They flew through the night for hundreds of miles, having set their course by the stars and by an inner compass. In the early morning light, they sensed that they were near the place they remembered, and looked for the hills and trees that marked last winter's refuge. And now, above the autumn chatter of the woodpeckers and crows, I hear them pour that pensiveness distilled, the refined and wild silver of their not-quite-ended tundra music.

They Have a Journey in Them

To the migrating bird something speaks out from the earth or sky with directions to guide its journey.

—Donald R. Griffin, *Bird Migration*

Once you recognize these two sparrows by sight (the crowns), sound (songs that begin with high, drawn-out whistles), and behavior (ground-feeding flocks), you will discover them to be ubiquitous components of the autumn landscape, appearing in late September, becoming numerous in October, and remaining so until April and May, during which months they gradually depart. This is the first thing to be aware of: the crowned sparrows are winter visitors, migrants who arrive in autumn. So are most ducks and shorebirds in California, as well as a diverse array of songbirds, but we have no other winter birds that are such integral companions in our yards and daily lives. The crowned sparrows announce fall's arrival more clearly than do any other voices.

California also has separate breeding populations of migratory white-crowned sparrows in the far north and in the Sierras, as well as a nonmigratory subspecies that lives along the immediate coast. But the majority of California's white-crowns are autumn migrants of a moderate distance that nest from far northern California to British Columbia, with a smattering of more orange-beaked birds that breed in Canada and Alaska. All of our golden-crowned sparrows come from the far north, nesting in high-latitude thickets of willows and alders. On average, the golden-crowns seem to prefer winter habitats that echo that association, favoring slightly wetter areas with denser cover than the white-crowns, though they will often flock loosely together.

Traveling hundreds or thousands of miles is hard and dangerous, so there must be substantial advantages. Migration allows birds to take advantage of seasonally abundant food (seeds, green plant growth, insects), as well as reduced competition for nesting sites and lower abundance of predators. If all birds simply stayed in California all year round, populations would grow until one of these factors imposed a limit. At some point food or space would run out, while less densely populated regions to the north would beckon enticingly in spring. Alaska is not inviting in December, but in June it provides everything a crowned sparrow needs: insects and plants to eat, uncrowded space for nesting, and a relative paucity of predators.

That's a key advantage of being a bird: long-distance migration is much more practical when you can fly. Even a small bird like a crowned sparrow is a tremendously efficient traveler, capable of steadily covering some sixty miles or more in each night's flight, or up to three hundred miles on a night of ideal conditions. (Most migratory songbirds fly at night, when they can navigate by the stars and keep cool during prolonged exertion, while reserving daylight for feeding and recuperation.) The physiological preparation that makes this possible is invisible to a casual human eye, but is proportionately astounding. We can measure it, if we look closely: one day the daylit hours cross a subtle threshold, dormant hormones come to life, and a number of biological and behavioral changes result. Suddenly they start gaining weight: in a week the sparrows have increased their mass by 25 percent or more. A quarter of an ounce might fuel a hundred-mile flight.

Think of the journey. A five-nickel-weight sparrow flies two thousand miles from Alaska to California. He flies through the night, thousands of feet up in the cold, thin air, hour after hour of pumping wings. We think of birds as small and fragile, and in certain contexts they are. But it is easy to forget the ounce-for-ounce durability of birds, which in many ways far exceeds our own.

And think of the magnetism, the fidelity to specific locations in both spring and fall that does not simply push them southward but draws them here, to your very yard or this stretch of roadside. Many songbirds fly alone and undertake their journey without tools or teachers. The night sky provides the clearest orientation: they are born knowing the stars. But many birds can migrate even on cloudy nights because they can see things we cannot: crowned sparrows and others have magnetically sensitive particles in their brain, an inner compass that always points the way to go. As they draw near their final destination, they search and find the visible landmarks they remember, which will guide them to their winter home.

September comes, and I hear their return to California: they taste our warmth and plenty, and sing as if they've just discovered spring. Then one day soon I see them, humble forms that scurry among the bushes as I skid over the gravel on the path to work. They don't seem like great champions of flight, not like the summer swallows, or like the sandpipers and plovers that outpaced them by a month or more in their voyage from the north. They hop and scratch and hide among the bushes, but I know they have a journey in them.

And when the days grow long again, a sunlight-triggered switch will flip, and winter's contentment will be replaced by an uncontainable unrest. The stripes on their heads grow thick and black, and their crowns regrow in brightness. The birds around them start to sing, and the sparrows add their voices to the chorus of spring. They grow hungrier, eat more, and become larger than they were. Then the April night arrives when the journey can no longer be postponed.

Some think that sparrows are just little birds, timid, weak, and grounded. But each will take off into the darkness on a thousand-mile journey away from home and away from warmth. They have nothing to sustain them but a few grams of fat beneath their feathers. They will sleep in strange and unfamiliar places, cross waters the shore of which they do not know, and face enemies they cannot fight.

The crowned sparrows see the stars and a polar glow upon the sky. They are freshly helmeted in their gold or white and black, fitted in an armor that gives no physical protection, but which signifies the courage that comes to birds in spring. They lift their high, shrill songs with an increasing sense of urgency. And from spring's land of seeming plenty they launch into a black sea of stars in search of wilder places.

Winter Crowns Still Mark the Kings

As noted previously, the basics of crowned sparrow identification are simple: if a sparrow has a golden crown, it's a golden-crowned sparrow, and if a sparrow has head stripes of crisp black and white, it's a white-crowned sparrow. During their stay in California, the gold of golden-crowns is generally quite dull, appearing as bright yellow only on some birds when they first arrive and some just before they depart, while the whites and blacks of white-crowned sparrows remain vivid throughout winter. But there are further and more subtle variations in those crowns.

At roughly weekly intervals throughout the winter, someone will ask me to identify the third species among their sparrows—not the golden crowned, not the black-and-white crowned, but the one with dark brown stripes on a light tan head. My answer: those are white-crowns too, the young "first winter" birds who have not yet assumed their crowns. Golden-crowns have a similar, though more subtly executed, evolution: first-winter birds may have a minimal, thin brown crown stripe, while winter-plumage adults have a thin *black* crown stripe. These thin stripes are much less prominent than white-crown stripes, except for on those arriving or departing adults in their breeding plumage of thick, bold black eyebrows surmounted by glorious yellow.

These are signals of age: I can tell young sparrows from mature ones. Can I tell male from female? Usually not, but it seems likely that the sparrows can. Both species are generally considered impossible to distinguish by sex in the field, but comparisons of captured or specimen birds reveal stronger contrasts (thicker black stripes, bolder yellows on golden-crowns) in the crown colors of male birds compared to those of duller females.

When I watch a flock of sparrows, then, I know that they are not undifferentiable birds at all—they are in fact among the *most* differentiable, and would be more so if I had perceptive sparrow eyes. They know who is older and who is younger, who is male and who is female, and they act accordingly toward each other. Although there's much I cannot see, I can perceive more of these relationships among the sparrows than among many other flockers: birds such as crows and finches are difficult to age by sight and are more mobile and hard to follow, shifting locations among the treetops. Sparrows are down on earth and stationary, sticking to regular feeding areas where I can watch them through the winter.

There is a flock of white-crowns right in front of my shop, for instance. We keep a few seed feeders between the asphalt and the sidewalk in the middle of a little landscaped refuge in this big shopping center. If I stand patiently and watch the furtive forms scurrying around the bushes, I find around ten sparrows on any given winter day. As I keep up my patience, I notice more: a solid half are young, first-winter birds, and they are easier to see, pushed out to the exposed periphery, while the grown-ups claim the prime central area beneath the feeders, where more seeds fall and where they are safely ensconced at the maximum distance from disturbing humans. The young ebb and flow: pushed to the bushes in a hurry by a passing shopper intent on pepperoni or makeup, then pushed back out by the adults they have intruded on. It doesn't happen in the opposite direction; young birds very rarely take space away from adults.

I can see which birds win the fights. Even more, I can see how the sparrows sort themselves in space *without* the need for constant fighting: the young birds rarely challenge adults, because they would nearly always lose. The occasional conflicts that arise when an outside threat pushes them close together are brief and essentially uncontested: the adult makes a little charge, and the young bird gets out of the way. From studies with banded birds, we know that the same thing is happening between the sexes: just as the more experienced adults dominate the young, slighter larger males also dominate females. Sparrows embrace the Falstaffian ethos that discretion is the better part of valor. Personal prudence is their first consideration, so they quickly assess their opponent's size, sex, and age, and react accordingly, even if those variables are too subtle for us to see.

This book began with the celebration of a nonflocking sparrow, the brown birds in their year-round pairs. I spoke of how their long-term monogamy reduced the need for prominent mate-selection signals: brown chippies have no colorful badges to distinguish young and old, male and female. The crowned sparrows demonstrate another facet of this phenomenon: mate-selection signals are often also signals of status in a flock. Strict territoriality and hierarchical flocks are two different ways of avoiding constant fighting over resources. Across the large diversity of birds outside the breeding season, flocks are clearly more popular than Nations of Two.

Flocking has two major benefits: increased safety and improved ability to find food. When many eyes are watching out for predators, warnings of danger are given sooner, enabling each individual bird to spend a smaller amount of time looking over her shoulder.

And should a hawk attack, a bird is generally better off in a flock, where the multiplicity of moving targets actually makes it harder for the predator to catch anything. Finding food is also more successful, particularly in the case of young birds who can follow the lead of experienced survivors. This advantage varies according to the favored food type and often influences which species choose *not* to flock: birds that cache (like the blue squawkers) generally prefer to have fewer companions, as do birds with limited, more evenly distributed food sources such as a certain class of prey animal, rather than abundantly clumping foods like seeds or berries. Hawks don't flock; waxwings do.

Living in a flock could potentially have its own conflicts as birds compete over particular resources. These are largely mediated by accepted status signals, such as the crowns of these sparrows. When new birds join the flock, there may be some initial exploratory scuffles as the pecking order is established, but the general level of intraflock conflict is kept at a very mild simmer throughout the winter. There is no hereditary nobility or divine mandate to these relationships, but the crowns the sparrows wear do serve to indicate the current kings with sufficient practical precision: a bold and gleaming crown is probably a bigger, stronger, mature male, with whom it would be unwise for a five-month-old female to start a rumble.

So the sparrows still wear their crowns in winter, to keep peace and order in the flock. We live within our human tribes, in which each member is unique. The sparrows also live in tribes like these, assembled from bold travelers who each survived a long passage through darkness and dangers. They are not mere identical and insubstantial little birds haphazardly thrown together for an instant. They find their allies, look out for one another, and share everything they know.

Disputing borders is for provincials, but these are birds who've seen the world, now come a thousand miles from their nest sites. They have left those battles far behind them. And so you'll see these birds you thought so common do something rare among our singers: stand beside each other, singing, without the urge to fight.

Autumn Kings Must Leave in Spring

The days again grow longer, and a wider chorus begins to sound. Hummingbirds dive in bold displays, while juncos and titmice start trilling in the treetops. The virtuosic mockingbirds and greenbacks compose anew their ever-changing melodies. And the crowned sparrows prepare to depart.

Their songs, heard intermittently throughout the winter, grow more frequent, but now have to compete with the great orchestra of spring. April marches steadily toward May, and the sparrows begin to assume their breeding plumage. I see the autumn kings becoming birds of spring everywhere I go. I see their change on my way to work and out my window; I see it in the bracken thickets on the edge of the meadow, in the fresh-leaved elderberry on the edge of the creek, and in the salt-crusted margin where pickleweed creeps up from the bay. I walk in the same places, but the birds are not the same: flecks of white come into the tan on the young white-crowns' heads, the black pencil line on the golden-crowns explodes into a broad brushstroke, and their tarnished copper caps transform into a brighter-than-goldfinch yellow. Their other home is calling, to which they will return with that same fidelity that brought them here to California.

They go to refresh the wells of song, from which I heard only the subsided levels of winter. The young will put on the crowns of maturity and make their northward journey for the first time. And should they return again, now three-time survivors of that transit, they will be done with deference. Next fall when they return and I hear their tundra songs, they will have traveled through a hundred dangers, sung to ward off rivals, and raised families, and will return now with the badges of experience. They will have earned their crowns and will take new places in the flock.

Every season has its music, so I listen once again as winter's song fades into that of spring. On a day of grayness and showers, I stop beneath the overpass that soon will fill with passing swifts, then nesting swallows. I look around at fences, abandoned furniture on the roadside, a puddle filled with broken glass, but even that huge mass of concrete overhead becomes weightless and inconsequential background. I simply listen without dissection as those pure whistles ring out in the aftermath of rain, and the dripping water rolls its slow tattoo. A momentary sound—once more those three descending notes. A glimpse among the branches—a crown now shining in the daily growing light.

Tonight the sun sets later than it did the night before. The stars are studded deep in a sky swept clear of clouds. This evening the sparrows take off into the darkness, and in the morning they are gone.

Their song is one of quiet places, and California now grows noisy with its lovely springtime clamor. In autumn the kings will come again, when the quiet light sinks lower. In autumn they will sing again, when my ears are ripe to hear them.

CHAPTER 11
IN THE DARKNESS
SHE WILL LISTEN

Great Horned Owl, *Bubo virginianus*

Step out into the cool night air and listen for the owls singing.

First summer faded into fall, and the autumn kings performed the coda to the birds' main months of song. But now December has come, and days can grow no shorter. Even the crowned sparrows feel the cold: their nesting instincts have disappeared into the past, and these days you rarely hear them singing. Now is when the great horned owls bring music to the dark.

Sometimes you hear a single bird pronouncing that unmistakable low hooting. Sometimes you hear a pair: he starts his stutter, and requital quickly follows in a higher pitch. Their hooting does not sound like the high warbles of the finches, so sometimes you will read of great horned owls "calling." But music is not restricted to the treble clef. Owls yelp and screech and whinny, but that deep and resonant hooting is their song.

As is true of other birds, song belongs chiefly to the early stage of nesting. But while you can turn an egg into a full-fledged linnet in two months, to make a great horned owl can take seven. The prey count must climb into the hundreds to yield two independent predators. Seven months from egg laying to a tentative maturity means that December is the time to start.

There is an early spring found in the winter twilight. The music of the birds starts in the lowest voices. The owls sing together when night is at its longest, for they do not fear the darkness or the chill of stinted sunlight.

In California, the manzanitas deck their twisted branches with cold December pearls. Owl song is like those flowers, impervious to winter. Both emerge while others sleep, and know the solstice for a new beginning.

The Hunter's Implacable Grasp

Great horns are by far our most widespread and commonly encountered owl species, versatile generalists found in a huge range of habitats, including urban parks and suburbs. There are numerous other owls in California, but all have stricter requirements of landscape. The screech, pygmy, and spotted owls stick to woods and forests. Barn owls favor open fields, and may interface with certain neighborhoods, but are usually not embedded in our streets in the way that great horns are.

Everywhere I've lived in California, I've heard the king of owls calling in the night. Sometimes the hooting is so near that I slip out of bed to seek it, shed the protection of my blankets to assume the protection of shoes and clothing. I step through the doorway, armored against the darkness, and see the bird that needs no such defenses: he looms on a dead and leafless branch, unhidden and unafraid. He seems to crouch, his tail protruding backward and those great eyes pressed forward as his ominous stutter sounds. This song is not a passive, casual action, but one of visible direction and intent, with his whole body in it.

I take a step—he swivels his huge head around, appraises,

deems me unimportant, and continues with his song. But something else sounds, something too subtle for my senses, and he stares now at something behind me and beyond. The great bulk of feathers lifts off, and from the quivering of the branch abandoned in the moonlight I must believe that what I saw was real, had mass and corporeal existence. Otherwise I might have doubts, for night is the time of specters, and the form that passes over me is a dark and silent ghost. He vanishes—there are other souls to haunt.

I hear great horns everywhere because for them the whole world is full of victims. Their diet includes a greater diversity of prey than that of any other American owl, usually dominated by small mammals, but with significant additions of birds, insects, reptiles, or whatever else is abundant in a given area. A wide base of prey means that great horned owls are well equipped to survive all year round in one territory, without the need to migrate. Their flexibility in feeding is matched by their flexibility in nesting, finding suitable accommodation in a wide variety of locations, most commonly in abandoned or usurped nests of hawks or ravens, but also on cliff ledges, broken-off tree snags, and more idiosyncratic settings. The last nest I found was high in a stand of eucalyptus. Red-tailed hawks had nested there the year before. This year the owls did not permit that.

Of all our birds, this is the fiercest. Some part of this stems from their size: their three-and-a-half pound weight is some 40 percent greater than that of red-tails, the largest of our common hawks. But great horns are less reluctant than most birds to hunt above their weight class. They have been known to kill and eat adult great blue herons (five pounds) and bald eagles (nine pounds). They will eat seven-pound skunks, disregarding the spray. They will eat fifteen-pound porcupines, disregarding the quills. They will eat their siblings in the nest and adult rivals who invade their territory. Small animals they swallow whole. For larger prey, their telltale calling card is decapitation, which I personally tend to associate with intimidation campaigns in novels of medieval warfare. This isn't their conscious intention here, but should I discover a beheaded cat, intimidated I will be.

The primary hunting style of great horned owls is to perch and pounce. In comparison with some other raptors, their wings are relatively small compared to their body weight, making them fairly adept at maneuvering among trees, but poor at efficiently coursing over fields for an extended period. Some birds evolved toward ever-lighter weight and increased efficiency; great horned owls evolved toward strength. Long-eared owls, for instance, possess a respectable three-foot wingspan compared to the three-and-a-half of great horns—nearly as large. But the talon strength of long-ears was measured as requiring 1,350 grams of force to open, while great horns came in at 13,000 grams—utterly incomparable. When they take hold, they don't let go.

The result of unparalleled ferocity and undiscriminating predation is widespread fear and animosity. Most noticeable of the owls' opponents are the crows, who will band together to drive out an owl whenever they discover one. But most birds, down to little hummingbirds, will join in the mutual defense known as mobbing, the attack on predators by smaller birds that are not being immediately threatened. The goal of mobbing is to drive off the hawk or owl, usually not through any plausible threat to its life, but rather through annoyance and discomfort. The attacks of hummingbirds and crows alike are a testament to the great horns' universal threat.

In the day, they can be outnumbered and harassed. At night, they have no fears. Not like us: we evolved to fear the dark and the strange voices somewhere out there. Now we consider ourselves protected by our walls and doors and lights. But a crucial part of wildness is that vague and ancient fear of the dangers of the dark, and we can still hear those terrors calling in this voice outside our window.

We can listen and shed our reasoned safety. We can reach deep into our bodies' memories, the memories of instinct and of prey. And when we see that great horned head swivel toward us in the shadows, catching moonlight on those giant eyes, we know that we are being watched, and it is not the bird who feels afraid.

The Watcher Sees through Evening's Shadow

Great horned owls are not hard to encounter or to recognize. They avoid only dense, close forests and completely open fields, but colonize everything in between, wherever there's a place to perch and room to spread their wings. Whether my bed was in the woods, the suburbs, or the city, I've never left behind their song. That voice is the first key to their identification: within our neighborhoods, this species is the sole author of hooting in the night.

If you should see one, its name provides the easy clues to identification. "Great" is appropriate for the clearly largest of our familiar owls. And the horns or ear tufts of these birds are usually distinctive, the protruding feathers thought to mimic broken branches and thus disguise their body's outline and enhance their daytime camouflage. (They have nothing to do with either devilry or hearing.)

Great horned owls are not difficult to distinguish from other owls, with these few pieces of information. But almost everyone can recognize an owl without being given any such specific details, because the group as a whole possesses a number of highly distinctive adaptations for their highly unusual lifestyle compared to other birds. There are a few species of owl that don't confine themselves to purely nocturnal activity, but their overarching evolutionary history is plain: the key undercurrent running through owl physiology is that they lead their lives in the condition we call darkness.

When we go outside at night, we feel an immediate loss of effectiveness: we can no longer see, no longer obtain the information we rely on in the day to make our practical decisions. Birds likewise rely on vision to find food, fight, or flee. And so it is that owl eyes are significantly larger than those of most birds, to allow the capture of more light. Even at a glance, the eyes of a great horned owl look large, but the proportional extremity of this development is easy to overlook: owls have been measured with their eyes weighing in at 32 percent of their skull weight, while human eyes are about 1 percent.

Some of their ocular adaptations have trade-offs: they are large and forward facing, to give better depth perception, but at the cost of the wide peripheral vision of most birds with eyes more to the sides of their heads. Owls are less worried about lateral sneak attacks and more concerned with perfect targeting of their prey. Likewise, they have discarded the sensitivity to the ultraviolet part of the spectrum that is common among most birds: the world of night is not one of fine colors. Even for owls, the nocturnal world is made of shadows. But what they see by scattered starlight, we would need a full moon to tell, and when that moon is shining, then the owls' sun has risen.

The moon, of course, doesn't have the sun's daily consistency. One loss of our electrified lives is our poor awareness of the nightly changes of the moon. I love the old poems in which Li Bai sees the moonlight shining before his bed and thinks it must be frost, Wang Wei plays his *qin* in the bamboo grove and feels himself alone "until the moon stops by," and Han Shan sits outside his hut reading sutras in the silver glow. You see things in the moonlight you won't see by the sun, quiet sounds are clearer when daytime noise has ceased, and patient thoughts unfold when visitors and obligations fade away. Now we think to extend the day with artificial light, and thereby often lose the evening, erase the quiet time between activity and sleep. Moonlit groves grow lonely in an age of off-and-on.

There is beauty in the softer light as there is in quiet music, and the owls know far better each rung that climbs up from the darkness. Not just the incandescent glare and its cold, forbidding absence, nor even the twilight and the noonlight, but each fine and precious sliver of the slowly waxing moon.

The Listener Can Hear in Any Darkness

The variability of the moon suggests the limits of relying on that light alone for one's survival. Fortunately, there are other senses, the most important of which is hearing. Owls do not echolocate to the extent of replacing their vision, like bats or certain swiftlets, but their hearing is significantly more acute than ours, and is vital to their success. Hans Peeters shares some examples in his *Field Guide to Owls of California and the West*:

> Upon discovering a perched Short-eared Owl the length of a football field away, it is instructive to pucker up and suck in one's breath sharply. This will produce a sound similar to the soft squeak of a mouse and cause the owl's head to whip around at once to face the squeaker. A captive Northern Saw-whet Owl busy eating in a noisy room, with people talking and the television turned on, instantly stopped and stared fixedly at a distant corner of the ceiling whence came the faint rasping sounds of a mouse gnawing.

It's illuminating to carefully imagine those scenarios in your mind. Owls can see in the dark more effectively than we can, but their powers of hearing are more important still for the initial detection of their prey. Of all the strange and wonderful things there are to think about in the lives of owls, I think this is what most captures my imagination: the knowledge that they are always listening and can hear the subtle, constant murmur that is just beyond my reach.

Listening is my favorite pastime. It starts simply and pragmatically enough—trying to identify different birds, for instance. And as the soundscape grows richer, clumsy chasing after visual evidence in a world of obstacles grows continually less enticing. I stop blundering about the woods and just lie down among the coyote bush, suspecting that I will hear the borders of the singing wrens as clearly as I can see them. But the longer I lie there, the more I realize that I was mistaken—for finding birds, hearing is not as good as seeing—it's *better*.

So many birds are out of sight, concealed among the leaves and branches, or on the far side of the tree. When I look through binoculars, I see one bird out of the three potentially visible to my eyes. When I listen, I hear all ten who are speaking, singing, or scratching, whether visible or not. And then I listen in the silences and hear the faint and far-off whispers that were previously drowned out by the constant scurrying of sight-sparked thoughts. Now I lay and watch the sky instead, and there are not ten birds but thirty—a flock of swallows chirping over the distant marsh, the strangled gargle of an egret somewhere out of sight, acorn woodpeckers laughing in a far-off, broken oak.

But no matter how intently I focus, no matter how patiently I still my body and quiet my breathing until I can hear the gentle pulsing of my blood, I can't sufficiently enwrap myself in silence to match the owls' hearing. And when I move I spoil everything, with clothes rustling, inhalations coming louder, and every footfall a painful indiscretion that overwhelms with noise and interference my own ability to hear.

To be a master listener is also to master silence. Owls have unique velvety feathers that let them fly in utter quietness. After years of practice at this birding business, I've learned to snap my head around at the slightest flapping or distant whistles from the sky. Alertness to sounds is key to finding birds. If a great horn chooses to announce himself and sing, then maybe I can find him. But if he chooses to be silent, then all my instincts and skills are useless. From time to time, our paths still cross, but not through any pursuit of mine. I'll be heading home as sunlight fades, listening to the night-herons squawking as they fly out to the mudflats, when those great dark wings suddenly flash overhead and vanish. I never heard him coming and see him only as he disappears.

Even more important than sneaking up on prey or clumsy humans who thought that they were hotshot listeners, this ability of silent flight lets owls *listen* without interruption by the passage of air over their own bodies. Soft facial feathers surround their ear cavities like the fluffy covers put on microphones by outdoor film crews to prevent wind noise. Imagine running down the street, unsheathing your weapons as you prepare to strike, and all the while maintaining a silence so deep that you can hear your target's breathing. That's what the owls do.

To see like an owl would be an extraordinary thing, to observe the impenetrable patches of darkness transformed into visible landscapes beneath a moon of tripled brightness. But if I could lift the human veil that sets the limit on any of my organs, I would choose the owls' hearing and listen to the faintest voices. I would know the authors of the nighttime sounds, their size and their positions, their chewing on a fallen seed or their step that breaks a brittle leaf. Every evening I would listen wrapped in a perfect silence, my airy feathers damping every whistle of the wind.

His Song Will Not Be Unrequited

Of course, the great horns are not always silent.

*Hoo, hoo*HOO . . . HOO HOO

The introductory hoot or hoots may vary in number or sometimes be replaced by sharper barks, before a longer, doubled,
and stutteringly accented note (*hoo*HOO). Almost all renditions
end with a brief pause and then two well-spaced, clearly defined
hoots. All the notes fall on essentially the same pitch: this is more
a rhythm than a melody. Great horns also perform assorted other
barks and shrieks, with subtleties somewhat beyond our knowledge dividing them into sounds of agitation, defense, courtship,
and begging.

In most situations, you are unlikely to confuse hooting great
horned owls with any other bird. The biologically quite distant barn
owl gives drawn-out, Ringwraith screeches, while the little woodland screech-owls perform higher-pitched, accelerating, "bouncing
ball" trills. In forests, you might hear spotted owls (a more yelping
and barking kind of sound, with a different cadence than the distinctive great horn pattern) or pygmy owls (single, widely spaced
toots), but you are unlikely to encounter either of those birds in
typical residential neighborhoods.

You can hear great horned hooting occasionally at any time of
year, but as with birdsong in general, it becomes more prominent
during the early stages of nesting. Hooting is also like other birdsong in that it is dominated by the contributions of the males, who
are more vociferous in their territorial declarations and defense.
(Males without territories, often younger birds, live a life of silent
floating until they are ready to wage war both vocal and entaloned.)

What is more unique to great horned hooting is that it also

involves frequent duets between the male and female as the nesting season approaches. One bird begins to sing, and the second then joins in within a few seconds, with hooting phrases alternating or overlapping. You can easily distinguish the higher-pitched female voice from the lower voice of the male within these shared performances. The owls also practice other reciprocal bonding rituals, such as displays of bowing and tail bobbing and classic acts of avian affection such as mutual preening and bill rubbing. As with the brown birds, various life history traits tend to accompany duetting—year-round territoriality, long-term partners, and little sexual variation in plumage. Great horned owls also live within a Nation of Two.

The female's specific expectations of her partner consequently go beyond the surface displays of goldfinches or hummingbirds to ongoing substantive performance—most notably the exclusion of other owls from the territory and continual provisioning of food throughout her several weeks of incubation and brooding. The fairly uniform hooting of an owl is not primarily intended to impress the female; she has already chosen him as the warden of her borders, a duty that he now fulfills. Hooting primarily announces territory, declarations in which she will eventually join her partner, to his great satisfaction.

Duets are not the songs of those who court, but of those who long have been together. As their children grow independent, the couple will pass more time apart, but now as autumn turns to winter, she tolerates again her mate's approach. Now the intermittent, tentative declarations that he gave even in July or in September find their meaning and their purpose. His hooting once unanswered now receives that higher echo, and with that validation his voice grows sure and certain. All his fierceness, all those deep-voiced challenges—now he remembers what they were for. He sang alone till nights grew cold. Now she joins her song with his, and the cold nights cannot touch him.

CHAPTER 12
LIGHT OF THE OASIS

Hooded Oriole, *Icterus cucullatus*

An oriole bursts into view as a simultaneous burst of chatter hits my ears. As soon as that chatter ceases, while my head is still turning toward the sound, he is already retreating, black and gold quickly submerged beneath the leaves of the overflowing mulberry. For a second he had clung to the slender outer branches, reaching upward with a steadying flap to pluck one of the ripe fruits, momentarily revealing his golden body and black face, wings, and throat. Now all I see is an empty, bobbing branch. A tendency to caution and concealment is understandable when you are yellow like the sound of trumpets. I could have seen that flash of fire from halfway down the street.

There are images that we remember and visions that stay with us. We are multisensate creatures, and can have powerful recollections of sound, odor, touch, or taste. But I think there is a kind of shock incandescent and electric that comes from sight alone, which blazes through our pupils to stiffen all our limbs and rivet our attention.

Vision often mutes the world, as when I reach the summit of a hill and encounter a vast avalanche of color, endless slopes of rolling green and wind rippling soundlessly through lupines. Or when in some mundane scrap of woods I find the first milkmaids that presage spring, and crouch down to cradle those white petals in my hand, see their gentle wrinkles echoing the lines on my fingers' tips. Even scenes that speak to all my senses—a meal with cinnamon rising from the bowl and sweetness on my tongue, a hand across the table and words I know have meaning—write memories that last in the lines and shadows of a face, subtle warmth and hesitation impossible to pin down with words, but speaking in a way my eyes can understand.

My memories of birds contain a thousand of these silent crystal fragments.

We each are granted moments when the obscuring gauze falls off our sight, and we see the world in more brilliant colors. These visions make life more worth living, and we wade through our washed-out days waiting for our shining hours. Some find these moments most in art, in action, or in the people closest to them. But I think there is a practice that anyone can use to cast off that fog more often.

It is to use our most fundamental sense to perceive the world that it was made to see. Not to live withdrawn within ourselves, but to open our eyes wider and let more of the world in. To listen, smell, feel, and consciously inhale all that is outside us is good. But if there is one sense that most often makes me forget the rest, it is this one that looks, that looks between the blue of the sky and the green of the leaves and the gray-brown furrows in the oaks. That watches and waits to catch the moment when another color makes its entrance.

A sound may give the warning, but it is the color I remember. I see that life in blazing motion that I cannot taste or touch. And the oriole bursts like a torch flaming in the night into the sunlit day.

Fire Bursts Forth

They chatter like blackbirds; the fire bursts forth on their
backs when they lift their wings.

—Henry David Thoreau, *The Journal*, May 8, 1852

Orioles chatter like blackbirds because in many respects they *are*
blackbirds, a branch of that same family known scientifically as the
icterids. Their particular genus is characterized by bright orange
or yellow (especially in males) to accompany the family black, less
social habits than most of the blackbirds proper, and a distribution centered in the tropics of southern Mexico. Of the thirty New
World orioles, three migrate north to California in spring, with the
hooded oriole the most familiar as a neighborhood bird.

Many orioles have black heads, or mostly black heads. Male
hooded orioles therefore stand out for the extent of gold that covers their nape and cap, giving them their name. In Mexico, they are
more often known as the *bolsero enmascarado*, the masked oriole,
which may be more intuitive to those not steeped in comparative
icterid study—the thing to remember is that it isn't the hood that's
black, but that their golden hoods enclose their black and shadowed faces.

That brilliant gold makes up the main color of their body, plat-
ing all the breast and belly and continuing in an expansive patch
above the tail (this is what bursts forth when they lift their wings).
The larger feathers of the tail and wings are black, so that the predominant effect is of a golden bird waving black flags in flight, or
of a golden ship that hoists black sails. Females are comparatively
plain, with grayish wings the main diversion from a fairly uniform,
pale yellow. In color, they appear roughly like gargantuan female
greenbacked goldfinches, but with long tails and thinner, slightly

downcurved beaks for reaching into flowers.

There is no equally tropical-looking bird in backyard California. Pete Dunne sums up the species as "an Americanized Neotropical beauty living in suburbia"—they look like birds who might be more at home in a Yucatán rainforest, where indeed they live all year round. When a northern Californian sees an oriole for the first time, the typical reaction is surprise. People up here don't anticipate tropical splendors in their yard and can live for a surprising number of years without noticing the fire hiding in their garden. Orioles get away with this by wrapping up their noisy colors within a cloak of caution.

I spoke in the opening chapter about how the brown birds are dull, blending in with dust and dryness, and so are comparatively comfortable hopping about in the open. To hide, all they need to do is to step from the center of attention and crouch in immobility—they have vanished. By contrast, any oriole on the scene automatically draws the spotlight and so must always be ready to dive into deep concealment at the first hint of danger. This is often noted by people who have orioles visiting their hummingbird feeders: step up to your window—never mind opening it—and the golden birds will vanish in a clatter of alarm.

Experts experience the same difficulties. Dawson's chosen epithets include "reticent," "secretive," and "a hundred times more bashful" than some others in the genus, leading him to admit that his impressions of this oriole's personality "seem to be very hazy," despite the nest in his backyard. The standard compendium of modern ornithological knowledge, the Cornell Lab of Ornithology's *Birds of the World*, is likewise full of fog. "No information," "no information," "no information" reads section after section, despite this being a reasonably common neighborhood bird and not some rarity of inaccessible jungles. "The single generalization" we can make of their song, the accumulated science of the world reports, is that it is similar to other oriole songs, but "markedly less conspicuous."

My point is this: bashfulness is not a surprising companion to unmatched brilliance but the expected one, the natural counterbalance to what might otherwise be excessively dangerous conspicuousness, were orioles to feed with such blithe unconcern as the dull chippies or the nearly uncatchable hummingbirds. Birds don't engage in heedless extravagance, but only extravagance compatible with their survival and reproduction. To host a bird of such tropic splendor here, it must also be a bird of unusual reticence and caution.

But those who shine have moments when their golden secrets glow, and you will see them if you watch. It is normal for people to assume their world inhabited only by such birds as they have known, and so that's all they find. Habits and assumptions are a leading source of blindness, but a moment's revelation can change all our future expectations.

You know the trees hold hidden fire. There is a chatter much like any blackbird and a rustle in the branches. You turn your head and postpone blinking to catch the moment when that spark is kindled. Then only one thing blazes brighter than that gold and black among the leaves: the glow of recognition, the flame reflected in your eyes.

A Palm as Paint and Canvas

A sound, a sudden movement, a burst of shining yellow—these things draw our attention once we expand our expectations. But there are always more astute observers, those who see not just the brilliant, noisy birds but the dull and quiet ones as well. Don't stop there: look for that which doesn't move and doesn't speak, and which is crafted in colors made to conceal. The sign of growing awareness is when you start to notice not just the flights of chattering gold but also what is silent and immobile. I'm talking about nests.

Once they notice them, most people find nests to be objects of curiosity and interest. I think there are two reasons for this. First is their clear identity as a skillfully constructed object—we can admire the intentionality, labor, and technique of the artist behind a nest in much the same way we admire a fine piece of woodworking. Second is the clear sense of a sympathetic purpose: a bird built this to protect her children. This is pleasant to think of in the same way that it's pleasant to watch a parent with a child, to see warm concern for someone helpless held above all other motives.

Most animals don't create such clear objects for us to admire. Most birds don't perform their parenting before our leisurely observation. But what we can see are nests, embodiments of both craft and care. As is true of many birds, the hooded oriole is both artist and protector.

Most neighborhood songbirds build little open cup nests of familiar iconography. Orioles weave unique, nearly enclosed pouches that give the birds their traditional name of "hang-nests" and their Spanish name of *bolseros*, or purse makers. These pouches vary in their details. Hooded orioles themselves are known for their regionally variable housing preferences, historically favoring clumping lichens in Texas or wiry grasses hung in various riparian trees in Arizona. But our California birds are not the birds of Texas or Arizona. They have a different way of living and have yet another name: 150 years ago, we called them palm-leaf orioles, and I think that title is the truest. Nothing more precisely defines our birds than the palms in which they nest.

These are not any palms, but California fan palms, *Washingtonia filifera*, native to oases of the Sonoran desert. These are considerable trees, the second tallest palm of the United States, often growing to over sixty feet in height and with trunks two feet in diameter. Their most distinctive trait is the hula skirt of dead leaves that remains hanging around the trunk, sometimes covering it entirely, though it is often trimmed in cultivation. *Filifera* means "thread-bearing," and those threads are crucial for the orioles, each of the large leaves shredding into long, tough fibers.

Female orioles strip those fibers from the leaves and weave them into an open-topped pouch of which the main pocket is some three inches wide and three inches deep. Most often, they will hang the nest in the palm itself, piercing the stiff fronds and flying to the upper and lower sides in alternation to pull their catenaries through, effectively sewing the nest to the overhanging leaf. Sometimes they will take the palm fibers to another nearby tree (perhaps a taller one, or one less exposed) and secure the nest either by puncturing numerous adjacent leaves or by wrapping the fibers up and over branches if something sturdier is needed.

If you have the skills, the setting, and the materials, then such a nest offers numerous advantages. The palm-leaf oriole's nest is not a typical open basket that merely contains her eggs and young, but an enclosing purse that conceals and so protects. It hangs suspended, securely stitched beneath the long, stiff fronds—not merely perched wherever chance provides an opportunity, but fastened where only those with wings can reach it. The huge, stiff frond immediately above forms a roof that protects from both rain and sun, but the nest is open to the air on all other sides to allow for ventilation in desert heat and make access by climbing predators more difficult.

On one level, these are instinctive choices, and praise of their ingenious effectiveness belongs more to the evolutionary process than to the individual bird. But I do not think that the individual who channels instinct should therefore be shorn of credit. Artists make their visions real with clay or paint, and they can't always explain the decisions they arrive at. The oriole grabs hold of her materials and likewise simply knows how she must use them.

She knows that she must pierce those stiff fronds and cling above and below to secure the pouch in place. What drives her to pull tight that thread? What compels the painter to lay down a drop of scarlet? An unthought and inexplicable conviction that it is the right and proper course. The building of a nest is a triumph of confident action over vacillating thought. Sculptors envy her assurance and strive for fragments of such certainty. The artist's great relief is to ignore everything outside herself. She needs nothing but the awl that she was born with and the thread she flew so long to find.

How did the oriole discover this desert palm, so far from her old oasis? She could not fail to find it—the artist sees at a glance what she needs amid the world's multitude of distractions. There is an image in her mind that she must bring to life, and it is always sharp and bright. She will fly past forests and past cities until she finds the tree at the heart and center of her vision.

The Vast Oasis

If we ask how it happened that she should find this palm here, in this place where I live four hundred miles from the desert, the answer must also include the fact that the palm was here because a person planted it.

Start with the beginning of the story of where the orioles live. This is the only bird in this book that comes in summer, generally moving north through California in March and April before departing in August and September. As is a common trend among summer birds from flycatchers to swallows, orioles move north from more equatorial latitudes to take advantage of temperate regions' spring abundance of insects, as well as, to a lesser degree, of flowers and then fruit. This much has always been the case, and is the pattern of all orioles in the United States.

But throughout the twentieth century, and probably beginning before it, hooded orioles have moved their summer limit northward. A part of this is related to food availability, as is true of the mockingbirds and hummingbirds that have made a similar expansion. The major enabling factor, however, is a very definite and straightforward one: our planting of the fan palms.

Originally, this was a tree of desert oases in Southern California. We then planted it liberally in the growing urban outposts of the region, in train stations and on hotel grounds and along the boulevards of Los Angeles, until by the 1920s hooded orioles were common summer birds as far north and west as Santa Barbara. As the Pacific coast suburbanized, we continued to plant palms, and the orioles followed: they appeared in the Bay Area in the 1930s and crossed the Golden Gate in the 1940s, eventually passing into Oregon in the 1980s and reaching Washington in the 1990s. Essentially all of these orioles build their nests from the fibers of ornamental fan palms.

These trees proclaim oasis to the orioles in any kind of desert. These are trees that stand for home amid whatever inhospitable surroundings. Donald Culross Peattie paints their portrait in his classic *A Natural History of Western Trees*:

> In profound desert loneliness they catch, each morning as the planet rolls eastward, the first fierce rays of the sun, spilling it in swords of light from the ribs and finger-like lobes of their fronds. . . . They have no company but the trade rats and lizards that scuttle under the thatch of dead leaves around the stem, and the liquid raptures of the canyon wren who nests behind the thatch, or the rolling whistle of orioles that hang their nests from under the living fan fronds upon threads made of the long fibers of the leaves themselves.

As I mentioned, the fan palms are often trimmed of that thatch of dead leaves around the trunk for the sake of cultivated neatness. But I hold with Peattie and prefer the superficial unkemptness of the wild form: "This thatch has a look of rightness and dignity," he says, and to cut it off "leaves the tree looking skinned and top-heavy, and, having lost its chief distinction, it now owns no superiority over other and more gracile palms." I relish the sight of an unshorn palm. That shaggy mass proclaims its wild origins at any distance, and prophesies the coming of the orioles who will seek it out above all other trees.

We have planted other palms, those gracile imports of the Near East, Far East, and the eastern states. Occasionally the orioles will attempt to use one of these trees, but none provides materials so fitting to their methods. The females who tear and sew those fibers know it, as do the males who come first in spring and know what prize they must secure to persuade the pale and slender ones to stay. The tree that they are seeking is a California tree, greatest of the western palms.

Some bird lovers assume that what we have done must be less good than what was placed by nature, and some seem to withhold their full admiration from animals not native to a place. I readily confess that we have made abundant blunders, but I don't think planting palms is one of them. I am unaware of any negative ecological consequences from the spread of orioles, and I think we can enjoy them in good conscience. Rarely is the line so clear between something we have done and the approval of the birds, and I embrace this job well done.

The fiery hang-nests find our palms and do not account them lesser trees. They reach my town and cease their travels, concluding that they have found a suitable oasis. Who am I to tell them they are wrong? Books may say that these trees do not belong here. But the palm-leaf birds were born wrapped up in their threaded leaves, and their mothers interwove their trust with the virtue of those fibers.

I wish for you to see the beauty not just in nature undisturbed or nature threatened but in the nature that persists and thrives. I do not think such joys will lessen anyone's concern for wild places or what is less abundant; I think they give it deep, sustaining roots and make it more persuasive. It is a great expansion of one's happiness to be able to enjoy not just rare birds but every bird. I find that the most effective advocates for wildlife are those who can prove a bird's worth not through argument alone but through their unfeigned delight in her existence wherever they should find her.

Are orioles less valuable for living in the trees we planted? I see the swords of light spill from the fingers of the four-foot fronds. I see black-masked birds of gold, brighter flames within that sunset fountain. And what spills here from the leaves is not different from what flows through them in the desert. And the wings that fly above the palm fly within the same blue sky.

CHAPTER 13
THE BEAUTIFUL PURIFIER

Turkey Vulture, *Cathartes aura*

The flight of a vulture is a beautiful thing.

It is effortless, almost completely unreliant on the tension and labor of flapping—to say nothing of the crude combustion we rely on to raise our heavy bodies from the ground. To fly as the red-headed vulture flies is to glide and to sail. Imagine yourself in a tree's upper branches, patiently waiting for the sun's heat to stir the night's cool air into motion. The morning ripens and then you simply lift your wings, loose your hold on the branch, and cast off into the sky as you feel an invisible wave carry you upward. You slide over endless miles with no more effort than the occasional shift in pose to stay in the center of those currents, those rising swells of air that form with the warming day, flow over the hills, and stream by in the great atmospheric rivers of the earth.

There are no other land birds to whom miles mean so little. For them, the earth has no obstacles. A vulture looks out, mountains and deserts lying before her, and feels no hesitation or sense of daunting distance. The long hours of a summer day exist only to be filled by that steady, silent passage.

Some might object that this tranquil soaring is just one fragment of their existence, and that much of even that time is mentally occupied by a less exalted object—the constant search for the tangy odor of dead flesh. We imagine their hoped-for meal and find the thought abhorrent, because their food would kill us, with our sensitive stomachs and fragile constitutions. Our senses are biased, but we at least have the capacity to intellectually understand this, to set aside instinctive repugnance for reflective appreciation. For when we consider the perfect algebraic logic of the world, the fittedness of form to fill nature's every need, the feeding of a vulture is also beautiful. No other animal approaches our great scavenger's effectiveness at finding the world's deceased and redistributing their matter, returning their cold carbon to the great reservoirs of life-to-be.

"Turkey vulture" is an unfortunately commonplace and dismissive name. *Cathartes aura* is their more fitting formal title: the cleanser on the wind. Once the energy of the sun has been changed from plant to animal, any being is suitable material for the vulture's cathartic conversion: insect or amphibian, bird, mammal, or man. Vultures come from the sky, sensing their opportunities from impossible distances. They taste the call within the wind and instantly assemble. And inside a day's short span, they return the dead to life.

Master Scavengers Are Master Flyers

If you want to make the case for vulturine beauty, their flight abilities alone form a fully sufficient response, as Robinson Jeffers, poet of the California coast, suggests:

> But how beautiful he looked, gliding down
> On those great sails; how beautiful he looked, veering
> away in the sea-light over the precipice.

When close enough, I can see colors: the unfeathered red of adult heads, the silver and black of the underwings. But at any distance, I can catch their unmistakable melody of motion. The lyrics go like this:

> Hold your wings in a V—each one at its fine-tuned angle.
> Hold them steady—flapping is for those who hurry.
> And if the day is cool and windless,
> Rock and tilt and teeter to catch each whisper of the air.

The more you watch vultures fly, the more deeply you absorb their extreme development toward efficiency, toward expending the least possible energy in keeping aloft. This is a key to their massively successful ecological strategy. Turkey vultures are the preeminent American scavenger in large part because of this aptitude for patient, wide-ranging flights that give them access to a far greater geographical space than mammal or invertebrate competitors: a vulture can cover a hundred miles in a day. As Bernd Heinrich puts it, soaring "has nearly the same metabolic cost as perching—it's the equivalent of perching in the sky." The beauty of effortless soaring is not simply that it *looks* easy and unstrenuous, but that it truly is.

In part, this invaluable efficiency is a product of vultures' basic physical characteristics. Wide wings and a light weight make it easier to stay airborne: their wingspan can reach six feet; their weight averages around four pounds. This is roughly half the wing loading of most hawks and eagles. Or compare this to human mass: we might weigh some forty times as much as a vulture. To give us proportionately expansive wings, we would require, according to my napkin scribblings, a forty-foot wingspan with six-foot flight feathers. With wings like that, I could imagine spreading my arms and feeling myself lifted by the swelling current.

A large wingspan—an adaptation favoring efficiency over agility—is one of the most fundamental evolutionary strategies of flying scavengers whose food is widely dispersed, intermittent, immobile, and not too small. When their food was bigger, the scavengers were bigger too. Once there were pterosaurs with wings of thirty feet that fed on the dinosaurs, succeeded by teratorns with wings of twenty feet that fed on our now extinct mammalian megafauna. We are fortunate in California that we can still see condors on their great sails of ten-foot wings, the condors who once roamed the continent. But the turkey vulture is the survivor, fitted for the shrunken world we live in now.

Vultures' efficient flight is a product not just of size but also of skill. Each day, the sun's warmth creates rising thermals. Air that runs into hills and ridges must go upward, lifting flying raptors with it. But even in cool weather, flat topographies, and low altitudes, in conditions where even the soaring hawks are constrained to flap if they would fly, the turkey vulture excels in squeezing every available drop of lift out of the air. That is the purpose of their distinctively wobbly, rocking, tipsy flight style, dubbed "contorted soaring" by the scientists: these constant shifts in position use each wing in alternation to gather up each little ripple of passing turbulence. The flying scavenger's core credo applies to flesh and wind alike: waste nothing.

And so the graceful glider sees our hills and mountains as springs of energy, as ramps for rolling waves that launch her from the land. And even when the air is cool and the ridges fade to plains, when eagles grow clumsy and strain their wings against earth's pull, the vulture tilts and teeters to coax out each sky-breath wrinkle and turn it into flight.

Pilgrims Pass, but the Gliders
Do Not Leave Us

The most essential thing to remember about this beautiful efficiency of flight is its fundamental importance in vultures' daily lives: patient movement is a key power of any master scavenger. But flight, that most essential miracle of birds, has other facets worth reflecting on. From our observers' perspective, not least of these is how it allows us to see vultures at all hours: their default position is in the open air, not hiding in the trees like many furtive songbirds. If you wish to have more birds in your life, no matter where you are, all you need to do is look up and search out that slow dance in the sky.

As far as the lives of birds are concerned, the other great phenomenon enabled by flight is migration. Not all turkey vultures migrate, but some do. In the Americas, it's the western population that flies furthest, moving from British Columbia to South America each fall. In autumn, we can see the pilgrims pass on their month-long or longer travels. As the host of vultures approaches the isthmus of Panama, they grow too numerous to find sufficient carrion, so they glide onward, fueled by wind and not by food. I imagine that great journey when I watch the vultures sliding southward on fall's long and fasting flight.

In some sense, our year-round California vultures represent the northernmost extension of the species' more truly southern homeland. Turkey vultures are resident birds throughout much of Central and South America, but are present only during the summer months in much of the United States and Canada. A century ago, winter vultures were rare in California too. But they have found our presence relatively congenial to them: humans brought livestock, wild pigs, and roadkill, while displacing many of the larger predators such as wolves and mountain lions. More recently, we have also done more than any other state to rein in the use of lead-based ammunition, a leading cause of poisoning of the endangered condors and their smaller cousins. Now we have vultures all year round.

Sometimes a Californian beginning to learn the birds will absorb a certain sense of belonging to a firmly Northern Hemisphere tradition, perhaps from the eastern voices that still loom large in our field guides and nature writing. It is easy to think that spring is the time when nature is alive, when flowers and insects burst forth, and when bright and exciting birds come from the south. But that is not the whole story of California. We are more Mexico than New York. Our winters still have flowers. There is still food to find for phoebes, vireos, and warblers. Our hummingbirds do not retreat, and the vultures too remain.

A sky without vultures is a sky unguarded and inert. From Washington to Maine, the air grows cold, loses life, and loses birds. Here too the thermals ebb and the currents slow to ripples. But we still see winter vultures, for we are not the frozen north. A whisper of wind is enough to keep the watchful glider flying.

The Sense That Sees through Trees

Their frugality with energy is key to vultures' global preeminence as scavengers. The low metabolic demands of their daily gliding life enable extended periods of unpredictable fasting while allowing them to cast a wide net for highly dispersed and ephemeral food sources. Numerous individuals share large, overlapping foraging areas within which they can quickly congregate when carrion is discovered. This much is true of most of the world's vultures. But our vulture has a second talent that is far more rarely found: she can find her food by smell.

The turkey vulture is the most perceptive of birds, combining the well-recognized visual acuity of the soaring raptors with an unmatched sensitivity to odor. The Old World vultures can't find food by smell. Neither can the condors, nor the black vultures of the East. The great majority of birds have limited olfactory capabilities and locate their food exclusively by sight. Among the scavengers, only this single small genus, composed of the widespread turkey vultures and their relatively localized South American cousins, the yellow-headed vultures, possesses this crucial talent. The olfactory bulbs of *Cathartes aura* are larger than those of any known bird. And that makes all the difference.

There have been studies of turkey vultures in jungle habitats, where tree cover makes sighting food sources on the ground difficult and in which the researchers made the challenge even harder, covering up chicken carcasses with leaves to hide them completely. When the meat was appropriately ripe, turkey vultures found twenty-three out of twenty-four of these hidden carcasses within a single day. (Give your carcasses a day to develop some odor, but after three days they become increasingly unappealing—contrary to popular prejudice, vultures don't want their food to be really rotten.) The mammals didn't find them: their individual territories are comparatively minute. The other flying scavengers didn't find them: they can see, but they can't smell. Only the turkey vultures knew where to look.

We humans are largely constrained to think in terms of our strongest senses of sight and hearing. But a vulture receives messages of equal or greater importance in an entirely different language: odors are clear visions and voices to this interpreter of the air. And so she looks down on an unbroken canopy of trees and sees her sustenance straight through it. She hears that silent compass calling and unerringly descends. Her world is overlaid with maps unknown to every other creature, paths of endless shifting odors that trail off into the sky.

A scent of death is on the wind, but one being knows it better. One graceful, floating figure glides closer and approaches, for what she smells is life.

The Life after Death

Let's come home again, to Robinson Jeffers on the coast at Carmel, imagining his ending:

> . . . To be eaten by that beak and become part of him, to share those wings and those eyes—
>
> What a sublime end of one's body, what an enskyment; what a life after death.

Flight is the red-headed vultures' most obvious beauty. Their sense of smell is unmatched. These are the two great adaptations that fit them for their role as the preeminent undertakers of the Americas, the disposers of the dead. But "undertaker" is an inaccurate euphemism. Vultures do not take things *under*, but raise them up in Jeffers's sublime enskyment. Properly speaking, vultures are the uplifters of the fallen.

Disposing of dead bodies is an enormously important task. As a species, we've invested huge amounts of time and energy in developing systems and cultural customs for safely removing human corpses from sight. To expend similar levels of effort to personally take care of the bodies of all deceased animals would far exceed our resources: instead, we leave the majority of their disposal to wild scavengers and nature's recycling. It is easy to find stories of the dire consequences that nations have faced upon inadvertently killing off their vultures, their corps of airborne cleansers: rabid dogs, exploding rodent populations, surging disease.

But there is a still bigger picture to be painted. It is in many ways the *biggest* picture: the natural cycles that encompass all life on earth, that ensure that dead animals are consumed so that their matter can be reused. In nature, everything is recycled. This bird is the planet's foremost mechanism for doing so: vultures are the most effective of the world's scavengers, and our turkey vulture is the most effective of the world's vultures. Look at the range maps, extending from Canada through the full length of South America: this is the most widely distributed vulture on earth. Look at the sky today, nearly anywhere in California: you can find this bird within the hour. This abundance is not chance, but the consequence of unparalleled ability.

Flying above a forest, in which a single animal died yesterday, the watchful glider catches that subtle flavor on the wind and flies directly to its source where others can find nothing. Friends and rivals watch from across that superterranean network of soaring sentinels, spot the beacon of that newly purposeful individual, and instantly congregate to fill this need of nature. In a handful of hours, the vultures have redistributed those dead cells and returned them to nature's cycles.

Many find the contemplation of death and its aftermath unpleasant, or unfitted for discussion in such banal terms of scavengers and their techniques. But if we want not just to rehabilitate this bird from common prejudice but to celebrate her, then the subject must be broached. We shouldn't let old habits of fear and distaste disguise the truth.

I stand with the ancient philosophers who amid their many divergences agreed in this: there is no torturous afterlife to dread. I stand with Montaigne, who believed that the final transition is no more to be feared than the passage from waking life to sleep. I stand with Ivan Illich, who found in much of our medical wrangling a fruitless fight against our mortal nature, fed more by marketing and cultural constructs than by permanent realities.

And most of all I stand with the vultures, who embrace and enact the beautiful circularity of life. They have seen death in all its guises, know the final equivalence of the departed. Everyone returns to the soil, perhaps carried upward one last time. To fight against the easy nature of this destiny is to suffer from superfluous distress.

My lifelong hero, Emerson, had a beloved and influential aunt who excelled him in self-reliance, the unconformable Mary Moody Emerson. Among her numerous impatiences with convention was her lack of timidity before death, which her devoted eulogist considered one of the "Muses of her genius." How did she respond when asked her opinion of war and the tragedy of lives cut short?

> If you tell me of the miseries of the battle-field, with the sensitive Channing, (of whose love of life I am ashamed), what of a few days of agony, what of a vulture being the bier, tomb and parson of a hero, compared to the long years of sticking on a bed and wished away?

She wrote this in a confidential letter, "speaking in the ear" of another favored nephew; it is not at core a political statement in favor of war, but an expression of her consistent defiance toward every attitude she saw as motivated by fear or polite sensitivity. To her, the vulture is a nobler alternative to bed and bier, doctor and parson, and all the other accumulated proprieties of cant or custom. This credo is clear: we don't need to be afraid.

The end of life will come, whether it comes quickly or at length, attended by nature or by whatever purchased trappings. Do we turn away from vultures because we avert our eyes from endings? The wind-borne cleansers are not the ones who cut the thread. They await the resolution and take only what's been left them. So if long years abed are not a continuance you cling to, and the ceremonies after death hold less weight with you than life, then that posthumous enskyment need be no source of fear.

CHAPTER 14
THE VIEW FROM ABOVE

Red-tailed Hawk, *Buteo jamaicensis*

Some birds I love to listen to. Red-tails I love to watch.

It starts with looking at the sky. It's always up there, the biggest thing in my life, an inexhaustible immensity that puts the little objects of quotidian existence into proper perspective. And often when I look at that huge expanse of blue, feeling a visceral release as I no longer confine my vision to books and screens and what fits within these tiny walls, I'll spot someone up above, some being soaring effortlessly through that sea without a shore or bottom. The red-tailed hawk is that spirit of the sky.

I look with my naked eye, as birders sometimes forget to do, and see the red-tail not in the artificial, claustrophobic framing of binoculars, but set within the vast unbounded space that is her truer context. I can't go anywhere without running into buildings and fences and prohibitory signs that trammel me in, but the red-tail has no borders. She flies to any distance, until she chooses to turn around. She rises and never meets a ceiling, just a thinning of the air as it continues toward the sun.

I look with binoculars and catch a glimpse of life far from this plodding earth. You can't really look at just the sky alone in binoculars, the big blue with nothing to focus on. But when I find a hawk, then I can see someone a thousand feet above the ground. My binoculars divide the distance by ten—now I am a hundred feet away, and so nine hundred feet from where I started. My feet are no longer on the ground and my head is in the clouds.

It's generally considered amateurish or old-fashioned to speak of the majesty and nobility of hawks in unqualified generalities. They are birds like other birds and not higher spiritual beings. Most modern nature writers aim for scientific respectability. *I* aim for scientific respectability! But sometimes I regret how we've become too grown up for eagle dreams and squelch our natural impulse toward admiration in a self-censorship of sensibleness. The coat of sensibleness can get quite stifling and burdensome, and I hope I never forget how to throw it off. Sometimes I think my only difference from people who find nothing grand in birds or trees is that I have a more weakly developed sense of personal naïveté or embarrassed foolishness to hold me back from natural enthusiasm. But I'll take a little embarrassment any day rather than give up my world of splendor, and so I let my thoughts of hawks follow where my instincts take me first:

I think a soaring red-tailed hawk is one of our most powerful images of freedom and rising above the trivial. I think to see a hawk at closer quarters is to see the strength that makes one fearless inscribed in beak and talon. And to return a red-tail's gaze is to meet something that is hard to find in the eyes of finch or sparrow: the immoveable intention of the wild and untamed.

Only Some Birds Reach the Sky

The red-tail is not just any hawk.

The other everyday raptor of California neighborhoods is the Cooper's hawk. I've seen their act a hundred times. I'll be watching finches at the feeder, doves trundling on the ground, perhaps the dusky demon strutting on the roofline with music on his mind, when suddenly the compact Coop appears, a short-winged ambush hunter hurriedly flapping into view. When he fails to catch his quarry, he flies to some low-down perch, perhaps on the feeder pole or edge of the bird bath. He catches his breath, then goes off to try again, to sneak up on some unwary bird down here among the trees and buildings.

Then I look up and see a red-tail. Not a short-winged flapper, but a broad-winged soaring bird. Her wings exceed four feet across, and she spreads them like great kites or sails to circle patiently overhead. She is bigger, stronger, calmer, less effortful, and *higher*. Red-tails are not little flapping birds, but fly like soaring eagles. For me and for most Californians, however, eagles are birds for special occasions. Red-tails are everyday eagles.

When you see a soaring hawk, the first step in identification is to verify whether it's a red-tail, by far the most likely suspect in most of the state—or country, for that matter. Adults have brick-red tails, but first-year birds have brown tails, and even adult tails are only clearly red when seen from above. If you're watching a flying bird from below, you can look for the "patagial marks," two dark patches close to the body on the leading edge of the wings. On perched birds, look for a lighter bib at the top of the breast, a relatively unstreaked area above a more heavily marked belly.

In time, you'll come to recognize the great red-tail at a glance when you see one soaring overhead. There are only so many birds that spend their days floating on the wind. Most birds merely move through the air on their way from place to place. Red-tails are at home slowly circling in the sky and can spend an hour going nowhere.

Sometimes they are hunting. Often they are patrolling their territory, a three-dimensional conception extending through several hundred feet of air. As they fly, red-tailed hawks periodically launch drawn-out and sinking screams, like heralds planting flags and sounding trumpets at the borders of the kingdom. You'll often hear these calls in movies, accompanying scenes of high mountains or of deserts, whether showing eagles or empty skies, because they universally evoke a sense of fearsome desolation. In my normal life, passed mostly here among streets and people, this is the wildest sound I know. The howls of wolves might convey a similar impression, but most of us don't hear wolves today, and think our landscape tamed and all paved over. Not quite: the red-tail's voice is still the fierce voice of the wild, speaking from the sky where its claims are still unconquered.

Sometimes he flies not for the neighborhood at large but for the one he hopes is watching: his mate, whether newly courted or reapproached after the distancing of winter. Birdsong is a fine thing, but even the greenbacks and the mockingbirds must seem small and timid next to a red-tail intent on displaying his magnificence. He climbs higher and higher in a steep roller-coaster slope until he crests the hill that he has drawn on the air. Then he slows and takes that breath before the plunge, three hundred feet through empty sky with no brakes but the wings he spreads to climb upward once again.

Sometimes she joins him in a sky dance, and then added to those climbs and dives are tight claspings of their talons. I watch this too, both unbinoculared to realize how those great looping flights easily exceed the height of my town's tallest ridges, and magnified to lift myself again into that airy perspective and imagine myself there with them: something drops into the pit of my stomach as I turn to make the dive, and down I race with wind beating at my eyes. The superfluous remainder of the world is shut out by speed and elevation, but the air I move through is no longer lonely air, and I feel the grip of talons that meet the strength of mine. I leave everyone below, except for that only one whose presence I find valuable.

Red-tails seem to use the sky as easily as fish use water. You will often see them simply stop in midair, not flapping, but holding steady like a tethered kite. This is not an effortful feat of strength, but the easy expression of control, turning into the wind and feeling it flow beneath their feathers. Other birds don't do this. Little birds fly through the air, but cannot rest on it. Even if they could, most would be reluctant to pause and calmly look around in such a position of complete exposure. Many fearful birds fly quickly; only the fearless rest immobile in the sky.

Scientists have tried to tabulate how the red-tails spend their soaring time. Hunting is not the primary objective: one study found that they flew for over 20 percent of their waking hours, but captured only some 3 percent of their prey from soaring flight. Courtship flights take up substantial time in spring (and lesser amounts throughout the summer), and territorial display and enforcement occupy many hours while the lines are being drawn. But red-tails soar in every season, spending time aloft that is not attributable to any of these definable functions. They use the sky for many purposes, but they also seem to use it when they have no other motive.

Other birds fly through the air to get to another patch of the earth. I think that red-tails take to the sky because the earth is of only limited interest to them. They will descend to eat, but the world below is tedious and quarrelsome. To fly on those broad wings is hardly more difficult than to perch, and up above there are no crows or people to interrupt their conversations with the wind.

Some sticklers might call such speculations fanciful and ungrounded. I don't know exactly what the red-tail feels, but I won't deny the existence of everything I can't define: it seems very reasonable to guess that flight feels different from what we know, and I suspect that it feels good. I know that when I follow a red-tail's rising flight, feel my vision rising toward the sun and the wind beneath my feathers, then I find my own thoughts soaring out of the rutted dirt. This interior ascension comes on me more often when I watch hawks than when I walk on my human feet. I don't know what's in the red-tail's mind. But my personal conclusion is that to elevate my thinking, I can't do better than to fly on the red-tail's wings. Call my speculations poorly grounded if you are one who clings to anchors—ungrounded is where I want to be, and I will get there how I can.

Red-tails hunt from altitudes that their prey cannot understand, and claim dominion over heights where jays and wrens have never dared to fly, casting loud, defiant screams into the untenanted air. They dance through the sky and clasp talons with the one who climbs to meet them, not at the mere summit of a mountain, but somewhere up beyond it. When they wish to survey the land they call their own, they do so where they choose and leash the wind to hold them. And when they have satisfied their needs on earth, they ascend and pass their time alone with the sky and sun.

Descended but Not Diminished

For the most part, however, we don't live up there. We live down on earth, and when the red-tails descend to a nearer proximity, we get a better chance to appreciate qualities that may not proclaim themselves so clearly when our subject is a half-mile up in the sky. And they do come down—the main hunting style of red-tailed hawks is not based on flight but on "perch and pounce" like the great horns, waiting on utility poles and towers, trees and fence lines. Here we see them closer, and in that more intimate vision, we gain a fuller grasp of their patient power and inescapable isolation.

When I see a perching red-tail, embodied in a landscape, I get a better sense of her substantial size. The next most common hawks seen from California yards are Cooper's and sharp-shinned hawks, those little flapping ambush hunters that weigh respectively around a pound and around five ounces. Red-tails weigh two-and-a-half pounds and have wingspans of some fifty inches, approaching human scale. These are big hawks.

Look closer. So many birds' unfeathered feet look like fragile twigs, but not the red-tail's talons, which strike and squeeze until the jackrabbit or snake gives up his futile struggle. Her beak is equally uncompromising, with an upper edge that cuts and pierces and a lower one that grips, the two parts of this vise sufficient to tear through feathers, scales, or fur. Above all this you see her eyes, grand and golden on young birds, maturing to a dark hardness touched with copper like the moon in full eclipse. You generally can't lock eyes with some flitting little songbird, but red-tails are large enough, large-eyed enough, and more than sufficiently self-possessed to return your gaze. A huge black pupil takes in the world like a spotlight in reverse, focused and undeviating.

The acuity of raptor sight is proverbial—"eagle-eyed," we say. I remember my first serious watching of birds, observing a pair of red-tails who perched in the tall transmission towers that ran through the hills near my teenage home. I could hardly make them out up there, yet I saw one descend from the summit of that tower in an unerring line to plunge into the tall obscuring grass and emerge a moment later with a three-foot king snake in her talons. I couldn't have seen her prey from ten feet in the air, let alone a hundred. Following that encounter, I promptly signed on for a ten-year stint as a hawk migration counter and permanent disciple of the raptors.

Red-tail vision is as impressive as that of owls, optimized to overcome not darkness but distance, the second of the major features of the world that set a limit to sight. Owls see what we cannot after the sun goes down; red-tails see what we are blind to even when the sun is shining.

It's worth reflecting on how this way of passing one's time—perching out in the open, alone and immobile for hour after hour—is fundamentally different from that of most of the birds I've talked of. Little birds spend their time in industrious alertness, always watching out and rarely holding still. Implicit in this contrast is the consequence of size and power: red-tails' lives are not shaped by fear as are those of the little birds. They have very few predators. This doesn't mean they don't have enemies.

Most notable of these are the crows, who as a tribe have an ancient enmity toward all raptors, an evolutionarily intelligent tendency to engage in proactive group defense. I discussed this in past chapters, how the corvids will summon friends and allies to cooperatively harass hawks or owls with loud alarms and dives that turn aside at the last moment. The crows generally can't hurt the hawk, but they can make her daily routine quite impossible until she leaves the area for some peace. Nor does the hawk usually hurt the crows in these situations—they are too alert and agile, clever and cautious. Other birds may also mob hawks, sometimes as a mixed-species flock, sometimes as a pair or single aggressive territory holder, on the same basis of alert, intentional action being much lower risk than the complacency that invites an unexpected attack.

Sometimes I admire the crows' community and coordination when I encounter such a scene. But what more often stands out in my mind is the hawk that stands alone.

Isolation is not measured in numbers and proximity. I often

walk with only trees and wish for no companion. When the red-tail soars above alone, I imagine her content. But the friendlessness that most calls for courage is the kind encountered in a crowd. Those are the lonely moments that more often daunted me.

But when the red-tail hears the calling crows, I doubt she feels herself cast out, for their language simply is not hers. She does not know their words for fear. And so when she receives the mob's mistrust, she may crouch, but never cowers. She may fly off, but never flees.

I remember one rainy day when even most birds sought shelter. I walked out on the edge of a new neighborhood, built at the base of rolling hills where kites and kestrels hunted. I huddled in my jacket's hood and watched a red-tail perched on a fence in the downpour, armored only in her feathers. She watched the flooding earth with eyes that saw through the falling water.

I like to get cold and wet and daunted, and then at my lowest seek that always undaunted vision. I love to watch her flex her talons and turn her eye toward me, see her beak in scimitar profile. Other birds can cheer you on a sunny day of spring, with their colors and their songs. But in the red-tail's eyes I know I'll find a strength that does not dwindle. The season and the weather and the events of passing days are minor things to the always patient watcher. I see that granite presence, buffeted by rain or raven, and see the immovable defiant wild, descended but not diminished, outnumbered and alone, alone but without fear.

What but Hunger Forged Those Eyes?

Size, ferocity, and solitude are largely definitional traits of the animals that live by killing. That underlying occupation causes some civilized and humane people to hesitate in their wholehearted admiration. But there is no real world without those truths, and if you would love this world you're in, then you have to love them too.

The first step toward an acceptance of predators is to recognize that those traits that I instinctively admire in red-tails are not mere fortuitous characteristics, but are firmly rooted in their position in the food chain. Underlying everything that I've described here—red-tails' wide and soaring wings, the strength of their talons and keenness of their vision, that sense of substantial individuality beyond that of the small and flocking songbirds—are long trends of evolution and ecological necessity.

Extreme developments toward greater strength and perceptiveness arose from the long, unending arms race between predators and prey. Size and solitude stem from the reality of trophic pyramids: a given area of land can support countless leaves of grass and perhaps a hundred finches, but only one red-tailed hawk. The fact that red-tails kill other creatures every day they can is not an uncomfortable disclaimer to our admiration but the evolutionary generator of those physical features that please our eyes.

The second tenet of predator acceptance is to realize that that same unending competition likewise crafts the beauties of their prey: no birds that we love would be quite as they are in a world devoid of danger. If those ages of pursuit made the red-tails strong and swift, such qualities evolved in parallel with corresponding qualities in those who would not be their prey: camouflage, speed of evasion, and the cooperation of the crows are all tied inevitably to those pressures. Jeffers idolized California's hawks in the belief that their violence created more beauty than it destroyed:

What but fear winged the birds, and hunger

Jeweled with such eyes the great goshawk's head?

Hunger, fear, and the violence of their interplay are real, central forces that have made an unseverable contribution to the splendors of the world.

And then there is one final quality that we see more clearly in predators than anywhere else, a quality that cannot be so strongly summoned without the accompaniment of threat and danger: wildness. I think it is an invaluable corrective for all civilized people to remember that a force exists beyond our codes and dictates. A taste for nature that extends only to those creatures we deem decently conformant to our human preferences will always be an incomplete and watered-down view.

Aldo Leopold addresses this untamable essence of predators in an iconic passage from *A Sand County Almanac*. He describes his participation as a young man in a wolf hunt, a standard pro-hunter practice at the time, and tells of how he came up to his party's quarry in time to see "the fierce green fire dying in her eyes." Over time, he realized that extirpation of wolves served neither ecological health nor our own highest understanding of the wild:

> We all strive for safety, prosperity, comfort, long life, and dullness. . . . A measure of success in this is all well enough, and perhaps is a requisite to objective thinking, but too much safety seems to yield only danger in the long run. Perhaps this is behind Thoreau's dictum: In wildness is the salvation of the world. Perhaps this is the hidden meaning in the howl of the wolf, long known among mountains, but seldom perceived among men.

Too much safety, too much loss of wildness, yields in the end a dangerous excess of dullness. Wildness, even more than wilderness, is vital—not vast tracts of untouched forest, but living, present reminders of the dangerous and untamed. I have walked in pathless mountain meadows filled with flowers unseen by human eyes. But by definition we cannot all live in wilderness, and to insist on that as a goal would be unecological in itself. What we can all do is find the wildness around us.

Most people will not hear the howls of wolves, nor see that fierce green fire. But we can hear the red-tails scream and see the yellow of their fresh-fledged eyes set into a tarnished amber.

I would not willingly choose the monotony of uninterrupted safety and prosperity. I want the world to keep its rough edges and not to dwindle to the docile and unthreatening. I am glad that I can look up and see a hawk who flies above all that we have built. I am glad to find a pair of eyes that meet my own with fierce inquiry and arrogance, unimpressed by my protections.

And when I feel more timid wishes receding from my mind, then I think that I begin to seek what the hawk desires too. I watch the red-tail high above, stilling in the wind, and if for just a moment I can hold myself there with her, then for that moment I see all that's down below in its unimportant smallness. She chooses freedom over things, distance over dispute, quiet over crowds. For that moment, I hold myself there with her, and the encumbrances of life, its luxuries and comforts, imagined obligations, conflicts over nothing—all flatten into insignificance.

The only things that don't grow smaller are those I carry with me, the thoughts that are a part of me and not mere objects on the ground. The only voices I hear now come from myself and the companions with whom I choose to fly. I spread my wings and rise in warmth that spirals skyward. To see things as the red-tail sees them is to see them from above.

CHAPTER 15
A LITTLE MIRACLE

Anna's Hummingbird, *Calypte anna*

Imagine seeing a hummingbird for the first time.

Maybe you passed a city-bound childhood in some northerly metropolis, or perhaps you spent your life on one of those less fortunate continents like Europe or Asia, old worlds equally devoid of hummingbirds. Maybe you read about them in a book, how in a far-off part of the globe there were tiny birds whose wings moved beyond the speed of sight, that could hover perfectly in place or fly backwards with equal ease, and that lived in places where flowers were always blooming. They sounded like fantastic creatures, something made-up and unreal.

And then one day you moved to California, as so many people really do. What would it be like to discover hummingbirds, to suddenly see in real life what before was just a wish?

Maybe you'll be walking in a garden, that day when you first hear a humming sound that you can't quite place. You leisurely carry your eyes up a tree covered in flowers, not quite aware of what you're looking for. Then there he is: hovering and suspended, beak deep within a tube of petals, before continuing his visits to one blossom after another, in fearless disregard of your presence.

Suddenly the bird switches from stillness to impossible-to-follow speed, chasing some other of its kind that you can hardly see as the two zip around the garden. The buzzing stops; the pursuit has paused. You spot your bird again, returned to motionless levitation, but now ignoring flowers. He is hovering twenty feet above the ground, buzzing and squeaking at something down below. Even from where you are, you see him shift his head minutely in the sunlight, see the rays dashing on and off those shining scales of amethyst.

Then he rises. Rises effortlessly, as if he's being drawn up by some great invisible cable. Up and up—a hundred feet into the sky, and you can hardly see him. And then that backswing and that wind-up change direction, and the tiny form hurtles downward as if it would crush itself into the earth like a willful meteor. But the bird pulls up at the last moment, you hear a loud "Pop!" at the bottom of the dive, and he resumes his position, weightlessly suspended and shining in the sun.

To live among such wonders is cause enough to come to California. There's no need for shallow invention, for the fantasies are real. I would cross an ocean to be part of this story and see the fables come to life. I would cross an ocean, but I'm already here.

The Intensity of Life

When I talk about the fantastic impossibility of hummingbirds, the immediately apparent manifestation of this strangeness is of course their way of flying. It is categorically different from that of other birds, with wings beating some fifty times per second in a figure-eight style that achieves lift on both the up and down strokes, allowing perfectly still hovering and flight in any direction. That hovering ability is crucial for both feeding and for male display flights, in which they pause in midair to sing and let the sunlight glimmer over their nodding iridescent heads. ("If I could only do that, all the girls in the country would fall in love with me," as Coyote thinks to himself in one Maidu story.) To hold still on any point of empty air is impressive, but what I am most jealous of is speed.

In the normal business of going from here to there, a hummingbird might fly at some thirty miles per hour. But when studying Anna's hummingbird in the courtship dives described earlier, researchers measured speeds as high as 60 mph. Such a dive involves a faster acceleration than any other known vertebrate and results in nearly ten gravities of force on the bird. Human pilots go unconscious at around 5g. This is the fastest speed recorded for a bird relative to its size, equating to 385 body lengths per second.

Those are the numbers, extraordinary enough as mere figures for comparison. But try to imagine what it would be *like* to move like that. You might struggle to run at four times your body length per second: hummingbirds can fly proportionately a hundred times as fast. Imagine dashing to the ten-yard line. Then reimagine bracing and setting yourself and hurling your body forward to cover not just the length of the field, but the length of ten fields in that same span of seconds. The world would seem a blur. You'd probably crash into something. But hummingbirds know where they're going, pull up and immediately stop to sing again or dash off in a chase: their brain center that processes visual information is measurably more developed than that of other birds. We watch movies and think twenty-four frames per second is a fair facsimile of reality. For a hummingbird, twenty-four frames per second would be a disorienting strobe light and an existence full of gaps. Her second is not our second, but something more vivid and dense with life.

It isn't speed alone that strikes us, but speed and smallness, the incredible amount of energy running through that tiny body engaged in such ferocious movement. I have some fancy ceiling lights in my living room that dim down to a gentle candle glimmer or ramp up until I can't look at them directly. A hummingbird aroused to flight is like one of those bulbs, except that my finger pushing upward on the dimmer switch would not reach its limit after an inch, but continue up the wall and through the ceiling as the light grows brighter and brighter and the whole room turns a blinding white.

It's this sense of increased intensity, of tremendous voltage running through a less-than-finch-size bird, that strikes me when I see a hummingbird accelerate. At full speed, they consume calories at seventy-seven times the rate of humans relative to their weight. My spectrum of personal exertion seems hopelessly sluggish in comparison: I gasp, get light-headed and jelly legged if I sprint up a hill and force my heart to double its speed. But I don't even crack two hundred beats per minute. A hummingbird rests deeply, plunging into minihibernation on chilly nights (known officially as torpor, journalistically as an "extreme nap"), in which somnolence her heart rate slows to fifty beats per minute. But then she awakens, flies, and races—and the pumping of her blood accelerates by a factor of twenty, exceeding one thousand beats per minute. A heartbeat every second becomes fifteen or more.

I watch a hummingbird moving diligently from flower to flower, when suddenly she decides it's time to go. She pulls out, hovers, looks around, then sets her course and leaves in a straight-line laser path into the sky. Compared to her, my fastest movements are wading through deep water. Compared to her, all other flyers are clumsy or lacking in vigor.

The mourning dove is fast, but seems like a bird thrown by the wind in a wild careening flight, or like a bird constantly falling forward, as if gravity had folded horizontally to press the dove in a direction she can't choose. The hummingbird is not like this: she's in control and goes up as soon as down. She is not compelled by outside forces: next to her the world stands still.

The vulture and the red-tail are made of patience and measure excellence in flight by frugality in flapping. The hummingbird is made of life and flies with fifty wing beats inside each ample second. She is a bird on fire, and blazes till her flame goes out.

The World Is Always New

We are citizens of the New World, and few things mark that fact with more clarity in my mind than the presence of hummingbirds—you won't find them outside the Americas. I enjoy watching tourists as they gawk at the Golden Gate or ancient redwoods—or at hummingbirds, our everyday miracles that are a standard perk of life in California. I like to relish their astonishment and smile in discreet satisfaction at my superior good fortune. Soon those poor people will have to go back to their dull gray worlds where all the birds are slow and graceless.

I find a similar delight in reading old accounts of Europeans' early hummingbird encounters. This is how the extravagant nature showman William Bullock described the wondrous Humming Bird of America that the sooty nineteenth-century Londoners could experience in his famous dioramas:

> [A] little being, who flutters from flower to flower, breathes their freshness, wantons on the wings of the cooling zephyrs, sips the nectar of a thousand sweets, and resides in climes where reigns the beauty of eternal spring. . . . There is not, it may safely be asserted, in all the varied works of nature in her zoological productions, any family that can bear a comparison, for singularity of form, splendour of colour, or number and variety of species, with this the smallest of the feathered creation . . . no subject of Natural History has, since the discovery of the New World, excited admiration of mankind more.

Indeed. I am quite tickled to reside among those jewels of nature that have excited the admiration of mankind more than any other creature. Sign me up for the zephyr-wantoning!

Of course, we here in Alta California are really on the periphery of the hummingbird kingdom. There are over three hundred species of hummingbirds, and I regularly see three. As you go south, the hummingbirds grow more diverse, and my Anna's, Allen's, and rufous begin to sound pedestrian in comparison to the crowned woodnymph and the amethyst-throated sunangel, the blue-throated mountaingem and the Andean blossom crown. Not just "hummingbirds," but emeralds and starthroats, brilliants and metaltails, woodstars and sabrewings exist.

Even those words are northern names. English is not really the language for the deepest odes to hummingbirds. Ideally, I would share the songs first chanted in K'iche', Guarani, or Nahuatl. The least that I can do is listen to the music of the *florimulgos* and the *besaflores*, the *aviapes* and the *chuparrosas*—the milkers and kissers of the flowers, the bee-birds and the rose-sippers. Here's Pablo Neruda on the flower-pecker in his "Oda al picaflor":

> To the hummingbird,
>
> flying
>
> spark of water,
>
> incandescent drop
>
> of American
>
> fire . . .
>
> you are a miracle,
>
> and you burn
>
> from
>
> scorching California
>
> to the hissing

of Patagonia's bitter wind.

You are

a seed of the sun,

a fire

dressed in feathers . . .

Here we are in our proper place—*desde California caliente* the hummingbird burns—not central and superior, but just the northernmost members of a fine and selective fellowship. And here the crucial essence of the hummingbird is also isolated as amid all his chain of fiery metaphors, Neruda centers on a simple statement: *eres milagro*, you are a miracle. For all my exaltation of the commonplace, for all my celebration of the brown chippies and the crows, I won't deny a miracle when it hovers in front of my face.

There is a ridge I've climbed a hundred times. I labor upward in late December, leave the winter flocks of robins laughing in the neighborhood below as I rise through live oaks on the northern slope, pass through the line of madrones along the crest, and emerge among great spreading manzanitas on the sunny side. All are green, as they always are, and kinglets have come down from Canada to find food among their leaves. White milkmaids in the morning grass reflect the miniscule white lanterns that drape the twisting manzanita branches in weightless profusion. Those hard and bony fingers overflow with treasure.

A gentle buzzing intrudes within the winter quiet. I raise my head to see the attendant of the flowers and bring her every impossibility into focus. Each set of petals is fused into a little bell that narrows at the mouth to keep out insects, because even insects are imprecise and clumsy beings next to this bird, who is the one the flower wants. Her beak looks like a sword, but it's not a sword that stabs—her beak and each flower meet like two hands that fit together. She holds and hovers, visits and withdraws, and moves in three effortless dimensions compared to which I have no up and down, only heavy flatness. And even this less flamboyant female bears flame upon her throat.

I live in an always-spring, where broad leaves stay green and white flowers tinge with pink even in the darkest month. The old worlds dream of lands like this, where a prismatic blur moves through the air in every season. But not all the New World has my luck. I draw a line east across the continent on this December day and see no hummingbirds once I pass over the Sierras. I live within the northernmost extension of the flower-milkers' pasture. The bridge from the south to me is this shining bird named Anna.

Anna's Quiet Glory

If you look in a field guide, you will see ten or so different hummingbirds whose breeding ranges fall within the United States. A few species have small pockets of year-round or wintering birds that inch across our southern border. But there is only one for whom these states represent the great majority of the year-round range, only one entirely and truly North American hummingbird. That is the Anna's hummingbird, and her home is California.

The other hummers of my state are all more seasonal and more restricted in their distribution. For the great majority of Californians, Anna's hummingbirds are the great majority of life's hummingbirds. Males can be recognized by their heads nearly entirely encased in iridescent magenta, appearing red from one perspective and black from another. Females have only a few such sparkles on their throats, while the rest of their fronts are gray and their backs a shiny green.

After speed, those patches of fiery splendor are the hummingbird's most noted trait in the Indigenous stories of California, reappearing in numerous tribal traditions as the extant evidence of an ancient quest for fire. In a time of darkness, Hummingbird is chosen as the fastest and most daring to travel to the east where the star-women dwell, to steal fire for the world. He watches and he waits, and then he sees a spark and seizes it, clamping it tight under his chin to bring it home. We have a native Prometheus, and I see him every day.

Historically, Anna's breeding range centered in the chaparral of Southern California, a generally hot and dry environment whose flowers come with the arrival of the rainy season, enabling nesting as early as December. As the chaparral's flowers were exhausted, the hummingbirds would fan out into the woodlands and up into the mountains in search of nectar. This pattern held more or less true up to San Francisco Bay, their approximate northern limit.

Today, Anna's range extends to British Columbia, with birds nesting in many habitats beyond the chaparral. What has changed is the increasing availability of nectar, primarily from the introduction of new plants—from ornamental flowers to winter-blooming eucalyptus—as well as the frequent presence of hummingbird feeders in residential areas. A hundred years ago, writers could call California "the land of flowers and hummingbirds," and it would be true for certain regions and certain seasons—more so than in other states. But today I can congratulate myself on living not just in the land of hummingbirds but in the age of hummingbirds, and I find Anna everywhere I go.

This is Anna's greatest uniqueness: in year-round range, this is the northernmost of all the hummingbirds of the world. Our bird has other claims to fame, such as those courtship displays described earlier, which exceed the acceleration and relative speed of any other bird we know of. Anna's plumage is also uncommonly brilliant among the northern hummingbirds, with the male's blazing iridescence extending over nearly his entire head, rather than being limited to a smaller throat patch.

In the early records of this bird in the scientific tradition, it was these shining feathers that stood out. That's what René Lesson cited when he declared it "one of the loveliest species of the family" and named his discovery after Anna Masséna, whose husband owned the collection in which Lesson found the type specimen. Lesson respectfully noted how our bird's eponym shared her husband's interest in natural history, and Audubon corroborates this in his journal, describing Anna Masséna as beautiful, graceful, and exceptionally polite.

Why was this bird named Anna? My best guess is that the namer thought Anna a sweet and lovely person. There are far worse sentiments to commemorate.

I have to admit that I find this extreme rarity of a female given name particularly congenial for a hummingbird for a rather different reason. Lesson declared this bird a great beauty based on the males' brilliant shining heads. The modern reports on Anna's hummingbirds all seem to emphasize the males' extravagant displays. I don't deny these wonders, but they are only half the story. There is a vital corollary to the incredible lengths to which male hummingbirds have developed their visual appeal: it is that their entire courtship is based on visual display, that their bond with the female is more transient than that of any bird in this book, and that they do not contribute to nest construction, nest defense, or care of the young. The corollary to flamboyant but practically absent fathers is triumphant motherhood.

I do not think the whole glory of hummingbirds consists of heads of molten metal or feats of airborne daring. I love to call my hummers Anna because it is the females I most love to watch. There are those of blazing red who burn brightly and depart. But there is also one of gray and green who nurtures and sustains. She sits on the loveliest of nests, a thing she built alone from down and spider's silk, until her chicks have hatched. She gathers all their food herself, until her chicks have fledged. Then she immediately repeats the feat, with all construction, incubation, and feeding performed without male help.

Flight, song, and color are all remarkable things. But equal to all those flamboyant wonders is a nest, the epitome of nonflamboyance. Hummingbird nests are warmth and comfort, safety and security stitched from the slightest things: tufts of willow catkins and fuzz of sycamore leaves, sticky silk of spiders and cocoons, scraps of moss and lichen. Those wonders of displaying males obey an evolutionary imperative: be visible. But the wonders of female hummingbirds follow an opposite command: conceal the nest.

Are flashing colors more beautiful than a perfect camouflage? Are dives and chases more to be admired than the endless patience of sitting still? For myself, I find that I by temperament invariably incline toward the quiet and the faithful rather than the brilliant and the boastful. I do not think a labor is more worthy for being widely seen. I think an artwork is most perfect when it fills a private need. And there is no work more private than a nest, art made to be concealed.

She approaches with no announcement and no glitter. There are only a handful of stars upon her throat, and the male's noise and fury are far off and forgotten. She bears another scrap of lichen to disguise the nest as just a part of the well-weathered branch on which it sits. And when I see that gray-green ghost perform her often unseen labor, I catch my breath at something precious in that silent, private moment.

Secrets are seldom told out loud. But if you listen and you watch and you hold back from overquick conclusions, then you may hear their whispers. The lives of birds are like their nests, hidden in plain sight to those whose minds are elsewhere. If you would be their secret-sharer, then you must bring something with you to the trees. No tools, or even knowledge, suffice to part the curtain. There is a little cup of down and silk, hidden in the leaves. The light that shows its presence is nothing else but quiet patience.

TOOLS FOR LEARNING THE BIRDS

Identifying everyday birds should be easy. We have more resources and better tools for doing so than every celebrated naturalist of the past. Choose a few of the most valuable and pertinent ones and you will be abundantly equipped to enjoy birds with the heady enthusiasm this book espouses.

FIELD GUIDES

The most valuable tool for learning to identify the birds is some kind of field guide, which in its most essential form contains two things: the birds' pictures and their names.

If you are just getting started with birds, I have one central piece of advice: get the most slender and locally focused guide you can find. For beginners, comprehensiveness of coverage is just clutter and confusion. Simplify!

Start with a Compact Folding Guide

If you currently can recognize fewer than twenty birds and are aiming to learn the common songbirds of your backyard, neighborhood, or local park, then you will achieve your goal most efficiently by using a compact folding guide that lays out many images at a glance. Such pocket guides contain eighty or so different species, which frankly is all that most people need.

For Northern California, two excellent options exist: *Sibley's Backyard Birds of Northern and Central California* by David Allen

Sibley and *Yard and Garden Birds of the San Francisco Bay Area* in the Laws Pocket Guide series by John Muir Laws. There are also similar guides to waterbirds that can be useful if you spend a lot of time around a pond or wetland.

Graduate to a Regional Book

Once you've learned the ABCs of your local birds—call it fifty different species—you may choose to advance to a regionally appropriate field guide, often on the scale of a single state or so. Such a book might cover around four hundred species. A good field guide will also contain valuable supporting information that helps to resolve trickier questions of identification, such as a bird's habitat preferences, seasonality, or key differences from similar species.

For Northern California, the two best options are *Birds of Northern California* by David Fix and Andy Bezener and *Birds of Northern California* by David Quady, Jon Dunn, Kimball Garrett, and Brian Small. The first contains somewhat less precise illustrations, but an unusually readable text; if you like to have a hearty dose of background information to get a feel for new birds, go with this guide. The second is a modern photographic guide, also well stocked with information, but in a denser and unconversational style; choose this one if you want lots of vivid photos.

Consider a Comprehensive Field Guide

Very few people, in a broad societal sense, *need* a complete guide to the birds of North America. If you are in that narrow subset of the population that aspires to familiarity with more than three hundred different bird species, then my recommended guide is *Sibley Birds West* (or its eastern counterpart) by David Allen Sibley. A seven-hundredish-species book like this is useful if you enjoy tracking down rare visitors, teasing apart variations of age or regional populations, or generally delving into the finer points of bird identification through masterful and precise artwork. If you don't need to do those things, a good regional guide is more than adequate.

App versions of most traditional field guides now exist (Sibley, National Geographic, Peterson, and so on), as well as app-only guides such as *iBird* or the free *Merlin Bird ID* from the Cornell Lab of Ornithology. Digitization generally encourages excess and its confusions. The most distinct advantage of app-based field guides, however, is that they include sounds, which can be very useful to have in one coherent and curated database. More on that in a moment.

BINOCULARS

The next most valuable tool for watching birds is a good pair of binoculars. Using a good pair of binoculars is very different from using a crummy pair of binoculars. If you've only ever used crummy binoculars, you really won't know what you're missing. What makes binoculars crummy? There are several variations of that lamentable condition.

They Just Are

If your binoculars cost less than $100, the odds are that they are not very good. The image is probably dark and foggy, and there is a higher chance of misalignment, leading to a headache-inducing exercise in frustration. Some investment is necessary to ensure quality. Fortunately, binoculars are like good hand tools or cast-iron cookware: they don't usually break or become obsolete, and it is quite common to use the same pair for decades with the ever-growing relish of increasingly effortless familiarity.

They're Broken

It is possible for problems to occur. For instance, if you drop binoculars, particularly cheap ones, on a hard surface, you can affect the alignment of the two barrels. If they are any good, the manufacturer can probably repair them, often at no charge.

They're Too Small

Binoculars are described by two numbers (8×25, 10×42, and so on). The first is the magnification and the second is the size, specifically the diameter in millimeters of the outer, light-gathering objective lens. Generally speaking, I would avoid compact binoculars of under 30 mm, which will give you a darker image and are more finicky and uncomfortable to use.

They're Too Big

The standard full size these days is 42 mm. Usually that's as big as you want to go; larger binoculars will be uncomfortable for most people. If your 42 mm binoculars still feel too heavy, seek out a lighter-weight model or try out midsize 30–32 mm binoculars.

They're Too Powerful

More magnification is not better. Stick to 8× or 10× (lower is fine too, but less commonly found). Higher powers are hard to hold steady and are fatiguing for your eyes.

The best way to choose a pair of binoculars is in a real store with many models to try out and salespeople who know what they're talking about. These people will also make sure you are properly positioning the eyecups (twist them out as long as you are not wearing glasses), setting the diopter adjustment appropriately (calibrate it once for the difference between your left and right eye, if needed, and then leave it alone), and generally not shooting yourself in the foot. Some bird feeding and nature shops have such helpful counselors, as do some hunting and outdoor shops. Others don't. Random people on the internet, or even random birders, are often imperfect sources of advice, since they usually are only familiar with their own binoculars and may not know how to use even those very well.

If you have no trusted advisor, what should you do? As I said, good binoculars under $100 are hard to find. If you go very fancy, say $900 and up, you will almost certainly get something good (though you can still make errors of inappropriate size or magnification). Between those figures, there are many good options and some less good ones, with the less good ones gradually thinning out as you move up the price ladder.

If forced to recommend a binocular under $200 that is widely available and likely to remain so, I would suggest any of the 30 mm or 42 mm configurations of the Nikon Prostaff series, which are generally lightweight and comfortable and give better-than-average optics for the price. Midsize 8×30 models are lighter and more compact than full-size 8×42 or 10×42, but do not play as well with glasses and will give you a somewhat darker image in low-light conditions, such as at dusk.

If you want to spend a few hundred dollars more, you can get something noticeably better. Even at this price point, there may be a better option for your personal quirks and preferences. But if you are just getting started and can't access a more personalized advisor, the Nikon Prostaff models are solid binoculars for the great majority of people, and you could easily do much worse. I will risk the impermanence of a specific commercial recommendation to save you from that fate.

LEARNING BIRD SOUNDS

In the chapter on the American robin, I explained several methods of learning bird sounds that you can apply to any species. As you do so, there are a few useful resources to be aware of.

Recordings

You want to use high-quality recordings that are representative of a bird's typical vocalizations. Most bird identification apps will provide this. If you are app-less and wandering in the vast wilds of the internet in search of a bird sound, I would recommend that you head directly to the Cornell Lab of Ornithology's All About Birds website, where the lab maintains a well-curated collection of recordings with solid written descriptions.

Note that it is generally frowned on to play bird sounds *to* birds. Remember what you've learned about territoriality: birds get upset when strangers show up in their neighborhood, especially singing ones, and especially during the nesting season. It's impolite to rile creatures up for your entertainment. If your sense of ecological manners is undeveloped, consider also the loss to your personal dignity: you don't want to be the one throwing sticks into the tiger enclosure to "get it to do something."

Descriptions and Sonograms

As described in the robin chapter, some sort of words, or sonograms for the visually minded, are invaluable in remembering bird sounds. In addition to the apps or All About Birds, which will generally provide at least one of those readable or visual accompaniments, don't forget to use your printed field guide as another source for descriptions to compare with the recordings as you search for your most personally memorable shorthand for a sound.

To explore bird vocalizations more deeply, the book to get is the *Peterson Field Guide to Bird Sounds* by Nathan Pieplow, available in both western and eastern versions. This is far more information than most humans need, but it contains both sonograms and the most consistent, accurate, and precise descriptions and transliterations ever written, for essentially every common bird sound in North America. I think this is my favorite bird book. Since the 1920s anyway.

FINDING BIRDS

Start by looking for the birds in this book around your yard or neighborhood and using your handy folding guide to identify other common birds you run across. If you then want to accelerate your learning and meet more birds, there are two good ways to do so.

Bird Walks

Joining a group bird walk is the sociable way to quickly see a lot of different birds and learn their names. Check with local parks, Audubon Society chapters, or bird feeding shops to find out who is hosting them in your area. These walks are usually free.

You might think that asking lots of naive questions will make you appear foolishly ignorant or will try the patience of your teachers. It's easy to feel that way with professional tradespeople or some brusque employee in a store. But it's different with birders: answering questions and pointing things out to initiates is their great pleasure in life. It gives them the warm glow of feeling knowledgeable, generous, and validated in their obscure passion by the interest of a normal person. So go ahead and ask them to identify every boring little sparrow—their self-esteem will sky-rocket, and they will inevitably form a high and venerable opinion of you.

eBird

For the less sociable, there is also the modern technological wonder of eBird, where birders all around the world post their sightings. Hosted by the Cornell Lab, this is the largest citizen science project in human history, and it's all freely and powerfully searchable at eBird.org.

If you want to see where pileated woodpeckers or lazuli buntings have been sighted near you, just type in the species name and watch the little pins pop up on the map. If you want to see what birds are found at your favorite park, just type in the location, and you can see both recent and aggregated sightings. Enter your own observations, and eBird can tell you the birds in your county that you haven't seen.

All this data can encourage some people to obsessively make lists and chase after rarities. Such listing has always been alluring to birders, with their life lists and Big Years and so on. The good news is that eBird can easily be used for saner, intentionally limited manifestations of this instinct, deepening your acquaintance with the birds where you live.

Explore places of recent sightings around your town that you have never visited. Become the eBird expert for your favorite park and visit it in the less reported seasons. Keep not just a list of all the birds you've seen in your life, a document most easily expanded by planes and cars, but, more important, your Five-Mile Radius list, which you grow with time and contented patience.

Group walks and eBird are very helpful and efficient maps to help you find your local birds. The best thing about maps is that they show you all the uncharted blanks between the road and the trails, the gaps in space and in your knowledge. Birds and nature contain inexhaustible blank spaces for you to explore. Look for that which you don't know, and you will never fail to find it.

Acknowledgments

Thank you to everyone at Heyday for making this book a reality, especially to my editor, Marthine Satris, for her skillful navigation of the line between challenge and support. Art director Diane Lee, designer Ashley Ingram, and marketing manager Kalie Caetano all helped bring these pages to life, while copyeditor Michele Jones gave them shine and polish. I am grateful for the beautiful illustrations of Anna Kuś Park, which make me feel like the opponents to the fruit growers' waxwing vendetta of 1908, who realized that they should stop talking and let people *see* the birds.

Many of the observations and ideas shared throughout these essays first appeared in varying forms on my blog, *Nature in Novato*, and in the *Marin Independent Journal*, to whose editors and readers I am indebted for years of support and encouragement.

How did all these creatures fly into my brain? Staff and fellow volunteers at the Golden Gate Raptor Observatory converted initial curiosity into enduring fascination. Early comrades at Wild Birds Unlimited, notably Scott Carey and Don Kimball, were my first resource for resolving avian mysteries. My parents, Michael Gedney and Shih-Po Hsu, opened a bird feeding shop and thereby gave me a passport to the best of all places for talking about birds with normal people and devotees alike, as well as acting as my first readers, encouragers, and poetry dealers from Wordsworth to Wang Wei. Corrina Carter gave me her writer's insights into the earliest versions of these essays, led me to the life-enriching study of old bird names—known to initiates as the Noble Art of Plumgudgeonry—and walked with me over countless hills debating the comparative spiritual merits of various swallow species.

Last but not least, my favorite chippie-chaser: Angelina Pavlosky-Anton was the finest of all listeners and heard even silent things.

To all of you, I am grateful.

Notes

Unless otherwise noted, basic information on measurements, range, migration, population status, diet, life span, and contemporary species names draws from the Cornell Laboratory of Ornithology's *Birds of the World*: S. M. Billerman, B. K. Keeney, P. G. Rodewald, and T. S. Schulenberg, eds., *Birds of the World* (Ithaca, NY: Cornell Laboratory of Ornithology), https://birdsoftheworld.org.

PREFACE

ix   **Aldo Leopold found it enlightening**   "Axe-In-Hand," in Aldo Leopold, *A Sand County Almanac, and Sketches Here and There* (1949; repr., New York: Oxford University Press, 1989), 70.

ix   **Lin Yutang gives a similar weight**   Lin Yutang, *The Importance of Living* (New York: John Day Company, 1937), 363.

CHAPTER 1: THE BROWN BIRD

3   **"Let us keep the most beautiful and fitting"**   Julia Ellen Rogers, *Trees Worth Knowing* (New York: Doubleday, Page & Company, 1917), xxiii.

4   **"[A] certain action of the parts"**   Elliott Coues, *The Coues Check List of North American Birds* (Boston: Estes and Lauriat, 1882), 61.

4   **"[B]landishing waggle-bottom"**   Epigram 10.68 in Martial, *Epigrams, Volume 2*, trans. D. R. Shackleton Bailey, Loeb Classical Library 95 (Cambridge, MA: Harvard University Press, 1990), 387.

4   **"Last week, our picture window"**   Joanna Newsom, "Only Skin," track 4 on *Ys*, Drag City, 2006, compact disc.

5   **Dawson, in his . . . *Birds of California***   William Leon Dawson, *The Birds of California* (Los Angeles: South Moulton, 1923), 403.

6   **"Brown chippies in the door-yard"**   Florence A. Merriam, *A-Birding on a Bronco* (Boston: Houghton Mifflin, 1896), 92.

7   **"The bird is a rustic with the stolidity of the peasant"**   Ralph Hoffman, *Birds of the Pacific States* (Boston: Houghton Mifflin, 1927), 315.

9   **"This overworked note"**   Dawson, *Birds of California*, 406.

10   **Only some 7 percent engage in these reciprocal performances**   Lauryn Benedict, "Occurrence and Life History Correlates of Vocal Duetting in North American Passerines," *Journal of Avian Biology* 39, no. 1 (January 2008): 57–65, https://doi.org/10.1111/j.2008.0908 -8857.04103.x.

10   **Duetting an average of seven times per hour**   Lauryn Benedict,

"California Towhee Vocal Duets Are Multi-Functional Signals for Multiple Receivers," *Behavior* 147, no. 8 (January 2010): 953–78, https://doi.org/10.1163/000579510X498633.

CHAPTER 2: THE GARDEN'S KEEPER

14   **"My pledges / sung in a voice"**   Ōya No Urazumi, "Kashidori," in Kitagawa Utamaro, *A Chorus of Birds*, trans. James T. Kenney (1791; repr., New York: Viking Press, 1981).

15   **Fistful of bird books**   David Allen Sibley, *Sibley Birds West* (New York: Knopf, 2016), 296; Nathan Pieplow, *Peterson Field Guide to Bird Sounds of Western North America* (New York: Houghton Mifflin Harcourt, 2019), 309; Hoffman, *Birds of the Pacific States*, 223; Pete Dunne, *Pete Dunne's Essential Field Guide Companion* (New York: Houghton Mifflin Harcourt, 2006), 442.

17   **Their mainstays are caterpillars and grasshoppers**   William J. Carmen, "Noncooperative Breeding in the California Scrub-Jay," *Studies in Avian Biology* 28 (2004): 10–14.

18   **Science by mass dissection**   Arthur Cleveland Bent, *Life Histories of North American Jays, Crows, and Titmice* (1946; repr., New York: Dover, 1964), 96.

18   **"I eat nothing but acorns"**   Edward Winslow Gifford, *Miwok Myths* (Berkeley: University of California Press, 1917), 328.

20   **Estimated their yearly caches at some 5,000–7,000 acorns**   Carmen, "Noncooperative Breeding," 15.

20   **They can retrieve insects and other perishables first**   Nicola S. Clayton, Kara Shirley Yu, and Anthony Dickinson, "Scrub Jays (*Aphelocoma coerulescens*) Form Integrated Memories of the Multiple Features of Caching Episodes," *Journal of Experimental Psychology: Animal Behavior Processes* 27, no. 1 (2001): 17–29, https://doi.org/10.1037//0097-7403.27.1.17.

20   **Store the other, complementary food items**   Nicola S. Clayon and Anthony Dickinson, "Motivational Control of Caching Behaviour in the Scrub Jay, *Aphelocoma coerulescens*," *Animal Behavior* 57, no. 2 (February 1999): 435–44, https://doi.org/10.1006/anbe.1998.0989.

20   **The jays who've practiced pilfering**   N. J. Emery and N. S. Clayton, "Effects of Experience and Social Context on Prospective Caching Strategies by Scrub Jays," *Nature* 414 (2001): 443–46, https://doi.org/10.1038/35106560.

21   **"Now the eagle, who was the chief of all"**   A. L. Kroeber, *Indian Myths of South Central California* (Berkeley: University Press, 1907), 224.

22   **How did oaks become the planet's most successful trees?**   Antoine Kremer and Andrew L. Hipp, "Oaks: An Evolutionary Success Story," *New Phytologist* 226 (2020): 987–1011, https://doi.org/10.1111/nph.16274.

22   **Oaks grow . . . nowhere without jays**   See text and map in Glenn Keator, *The Life of an Oak: An Intimate Portrait* (Berkeley, CA: Heyday Books, 1998), 137.

23   **In spring they will return**   Carmen, "Noncooperative Breeding," 40.

CHAPTER 3: I CAN HEAR WHEN THEY CALL

28   **"The world was made by Prairie Falcon, Crow, and Coyote"** Edward Winslow Gifford, "Western Mono Myths," *Journal of American Folk-Lore* 36, no. 142 (October–December 1923): 305.

29   **What John Marzluff and Tony Angell call an Eden for crows** John M. Marzluff and Tony Angell, *In the Company of Crows and Ravens* (New Haven: Yale University Press, 2005), 94.

29   **In the 1930s**   John T. Emlen Jr., "The Midwinter Distribution of the Crow in California," *Condor* 42 (November 1940): 287–94, https://doi.org/10.2307/1364161.

29   **By the 1980s**   W. Paul Gorenzel and Terrell P. Salmon, "Urban Crow Roosts in California," *Proceedings of the Fifteenth Vertebrate Pest Conference* (March 1992): 97–102, http://digitalcommons.unl.edu /vpc15/33.

29   **Winter roosts were dynamited**   Marzluff and Angell, *In the Company*, 91.

30   **Their . . . threat to smaller birds (which is easily overstated)** According to a 2004 review of corvid impacts, some studies of American crows show declines in productivity of prey species (fledglings per nest, for instance), but none show declines in abundance (size of the adult breeding population). The early life of birds is full of risks, of which crow predation in the nest is only one small part. Christine F. Madden, Beatriz Arroyo, and Arjun Amar, "A Review of the Impacts of Corvids on Bird Productivity and Abundance," *Ibis* 157 (2015): 1–16, https://doi.org/10.1111/ibi.12223.

30   **More at risk**   Sarah S. Wheeler, Christopher M. Barker, Ying Fang, M. Veronica Armijos, Brian D. Carroll, Stan Husted, Wesley O. Johnson, and William K. Reisen, "Differential Impact of West Nile Virus on California Birds," *Condor* 111, no. 1 (2009): 1–20, http://dx.doi .org/10.1525/cond.2009.080013.

30   **California's winter crow population increased by over 400 percent**   T. D. Meehan, G. S. LeBaron, K. Dale, A. Krump, N. L. Michel, and C. B. Wilsey, "Abundance Trends of Birds Wintering in the USA and Canada, from Audubon Christmas Bird Counts, 1966–2019, version 3.0," National Audubon Society, https://www.audubon.org /conservation/where-have-all-birds-gone.

32   **A sister plucked flower petals**   Carolee Caffrey, "Goal-Directed Use of Objects by American Crows," *Wilson Bulletin* 113, no. 1 (March 2001): 114–115, http://dx.doi.org/10.1676/0043-5643(2001)113[0114: GDUOOB]2.0.CO;2.

34   **"I can hear when he calls"**   Henry David Thoreau, *Thoreau on Birds* (1910; repr., Boston: Beacon Press, 1993), 258.

35   **Seen wearing the masks**   John M. Marzluff, Jeff Walls, Heather N. Cornell, John C. Withey, and David P. Craig, "Lasting Recognition of Threatening People by Wild American Crows," *Animal Behavior* 79 (2010): 699–707, https://doi.org/10.1016/j.anbehav.2009.12.022.

35   **One girl in Seattle**   Katy Sewall, "The Girl Who Gets Gifts from Birds," *BBC News Magazine*, February 25, 2015, https://www.bbc.com /news/magazine-31604026.

35   **Pet crows' personality**   Arthur Cleveland Bent, *Life Histories of North American Jays, Crows and Titmice, Part II* (New York: Dover, 1964), 246.

CHAPTER 4: WAXWING REVELATIONS

42   **"Beauty conquered"**   Edward Howe Forbush, "The Cedar Waxwing," *Bird-Lore* 13 (1911): 55–58. I've seen Forbush's telling of this cited elsewhere, but never any more objective corroborating account. It may be a case, as E. B. White wrote admiringly of the Forbushian method, of "leaving the reader to decide whether there is any truth in the report or whether it's a cock-and-bull story." E. B. White, "Mr. Forbush's Friends," *New Yorker*, February 18, 1966, https://www.newyorker.com/magazine/1966/02/26/mr -forbushs-friends.

CHAPTER 5: DAWN'S WATCHER

54   **"Red, Red Robin"**   Louis Armstrong, vocalist, "When the Red, Red Robin (Comes Bob, Bob, Bobbin' Along)," recorded 1956, by Harry Woods, track 13 on *Ambassador Satch*, 2007, Columbia, compact disc.

54   **"[P]iwío, pihi, piwó"**   Vocalization as rendered by Héctor Gómez de Silva in Kenn Kaufman, *Guia de Campo Kaufman a las Aves de Norte-America* (New York: Houghton Mifflin, 2005), 252.

61   **"It sings with power"**   Henry David Thoreau, *The Journal*, April 21, 1852, in *Thoreau on Birds*, 438–439.

CHAPTER 6: THE BLESSED HALO

66   **"The linnet is the bread-and-butter"**   Dawson, *Birds of California*, 214.

67 "[L]innets crack seeds at the feed tray" Gary Snyder, "A Dry Day Just Before the Rainy Season," in *The Back Country* (New York: New Directions, 1968), 78.

67 "[L]innets like wounds" Robert Hass, "Lines on Last Spring," in *Field Guide* (New Haven: Yale University Press, 1973), 22.

69 "So familiar and abundant" William Finley, "House Finch," in *Birds of America, Part III*, ed. T. Gilbert Pearson (1917; repr., Garden City, NY: Garden City Publishing, 1936), 7.

69 Mary Austin Mary Austin, *The Land of Little Rain* (1903; repr., New York: Penguin, 1988), 51–52.

70 "If your heart was like mine" Gary Snyder, *Rip-rap and Cold Mountain Poems* (1958; repr., Washington, DC: Shoemaker & Hoard, 2004), 44.

73 "A lighter and more exuberant heart" Charles A. Keeler, *Bird Notes Afield* (San Francisco: D. P. Elder & Morgan Shepard, 1899), 167.

74 "[T]he magic of names and poems" Hass, "Letter," in *Field Guide*, 66.

CHAPTER 7: THIS GOLDFINCH IS NOT LESSER

80 "Shades of Audubon!" Dawson, *Birds of California*, 194.

81 The jarring of cracked glass Hoffman, *Birds of the Pacific States*, 308.

81 "Gentle deprecating calls" Florence Merriam Bailey, cited in J. M. Linsdale, "Goldfinches on the Hastings Natural History Reservation," *American Midland Naturalist* 57, no. 1 (January 1957): 53, https://doi.org/10.2307/2422524.

84 About 10 percent of a typical song Sharon Goldwasser, "Vocal Appropriation in the Lesser Goldfinch," master's thesis (University of Arizona, 1987): 25–38, https://repository.arizona.edu/handle /10150/291759.

84 Staccato flight calls are used for *individual* recognition Paul C. Mundinger, "Vocal Imitation and Individual Recognition of Finch Calls," *Science* 168, no. 3930 (April 1970): 480–82, https://doi.org /10.1126/science.168.3930.480; Paul C. Mundinger, "Call Learning in the Carduelinae: Ethological and Systematic Considerations," *Systematic Biology* 28, no. 3 (September 1979): 270283, https://doi.org /10.1093/sysbio/28.3.270.

85 Thirty to forty different species Goldwasser, "Vocal Appropriation," 33; J. V. Remsen Jr., Kimball Garrett, and Richard A. Erickson, "Vocal Copying in Lawrence's and Lesser Goldfinches," *Western Birds* 13 (1982): 29–33, https://sora.unm.edu/node/122177.

CHAPTER 8: DEVOTION'S FRUIT

92   **Falcon's journey to the end of the world**   "Wek'-wek's Search for His Father," in C. Hart Merriam, *The Dawn of the World* (Cleveland: Arthur H. Clark Company, 1910), 184.

92   **Falcon again thinks he can outrace Dove**   "The Making of Arrows," in Edward Winslow Gifford, *Miwok Myths* (Berkeley: University of California Press, 1917), 303.

92   **Hummingbird . . . issues the same challenge**   "Lizard and Fox," in Gifford, *Miwok Myths*, 327.

92   **A. H. Gayton's survey**   A. H. Gayton, *Yokuts-Mono Chiefs and Shamans* (Berkeley: University of California Press, 1930), 386.

93   **"Zenaida is a vesper bird"**   To be precise, he used the genus name at the time, *Zenaidura*. Wallace Craig, "The Expressions of Emotion in the Pigeons: II. The Mourning Dove," *Auk* 18, no. 4 (October 1911): 407.

95   **A Yurok story**   Told by Florence Shaughnessy in R. H. Robins, *The Yurok Language: Grammar, Texts, and Lexicon* (Berkeley: University of California Press, 1958), 155. The story's prevalence, with some variation, among both Hupa and Yurok story traditions is described in Sean O'Neill, "The Howling Muse: Chasing Coyote Tales in Northwestern California," *Cahiers de littérature orale* 81 (2017): 159, https://doi.org/10.4000/clo.3209.

95   **"Their plaintive call suggests"**   Edward Abbey, *Desert Solitaire* (1968; repr., Tucson: University of Arizona Press, 1988), 17.

96   **"My dove in the clefts of the rock"**   Song of Solomon 2:14. *The Song of Songs*, trans. Ariel and Chana Bloch (New York: Random House, 1995).

97   **"Adore each other"**   Translation by the author. Victor Hugo, *Les Misérables* (1862; repr., Paris: Hachette, 1884), 293.

97   **Cooing typically decreases by more than 90 percent**   Gary L. Jackson and Thomas S. Baskett, "Perch-Cooing and Other Aspects of Breeding Behavior of Mourning Doves," *Journal of Wildlife Management* 28, no. 2 (April 1964): 295.

98   **Biologist Bernd Heinrich**   Bernd Heinrich, *The Nesting Season* (Cambridge: Harvard University Press, 2010).

CHAPTER 9: THE DUSKY DEMON

101   **"This celebrated and very extraordinary bird"**   Alexander Wilson, *American Ornithology, or The Natural History of the Birds of the United States, Vol. II* (New York: Collins & Co., 1828), 94.

103 **"[M]ake the vaults of America ring"** Walt Whitman, "All about a Mocking-Bird," *New York Saturday Press*, January 7, 1860, https://whitmanarchive.org/criticism/reviews/reminiscence/anc.00140.html.

106 **An estimate of 82 song elements** Kim C. Derrickson, "Yearly and Situational Changes in the Estimate of Repertoire Size in Northern Mockingbirds (*Mimus polyglottos*)," *Auk* 104, no. 2 (April 1, 1987): 198–207, https://doi.org/10.1093/auk/104.2.198.

108 **Known cases of mockingbird "sequential polyandry"** Cheryl A. Logan, "Mate Switching and Mate Choice in Female Northern Mockingbirds: Facultative Monogamy," *Wilson Bulletin* 103, no. 2 (June 1991): 277–81, https://www.jstor.org/stable/4163011.

109 **She will leave** Cheryl A. Logan, "Mate-Reassessment in an Already-Mated Female Northern Mockingbird," *Chat* 61, no. 2 (Spring 1997): 108–12, https://www.carolinabirdclub.org/chat/issues/1997/v61n2.html; Logan, "Mate Switching."

109 **Male parental investment is higher** Julia Zaias and Randall Breitwisch, "Intra-Pair Cooperation, Fledgling Care, and Renesting by Northern Mockingbirds (*Mimus polyglottos*)," *Ethology* 80 (1989): 94–110, https://doi.org/10.1111/j.1439-0310.1989.tb00732.x; Randall Breitwisch, Peter G. Merritt, and George H. Whitesides, "Parental Investment by the Northern Mockingbird: Male and Female Roles in Feeding Nestlings," *Auk* 103, no. 1 (January 1986): 152–59, https://doi.org/10.1093/auk/103.1.152.

111 **"Out of the Cradle Endlessly Rocking"** Walt Whitman, *Leaves of Grass* (1891; repr., New York: Modern Library, 1950), 205.

CHAPTER 10: AUTUMN KINGS

117 **"To the migrating bird something speaks"** Donald R. Griffin, *Bird Migration* (Garden City, NY: Doubleday & Company, 1964), xi.

120 **Winter-plumage adults have a thin *black* crown stripe** The seasonality of golden-crowned sparrow plumage has additional subtleties. It seems that the majority of adult female golden-crowns revert to the brown crown stripes of immature birds, but that some adopt the black crown stripes uniformly found in adult males. Rita R. Colwell, "Age-Specific Crown Variation in Basic-Plumaged Golden-Crowned Sparrows," *North American Bird Bander* 24, no. 4 (October–December 1999): 138–42, https://sora.unm.edu/node/93509.

122 **Young birds very rarely take space away from adults** Gregory C. Keys and Stephen I. Rothstein, "Benefits and Costs of Dominance and Subordinance in White-Crowned Sparrows and the Paradox of Status Signalling," *Animal Behaviour* 42, no. 6 (December 1991): 899–912, https://doi.org/10.1016/S0003-3472(05)80142-3.

CHAPTER 11: IN THE DARKNESS SHE WILL LISTEN

130 **Talon strength**   Carl D. Marti, "Feeding Ecology of Four Sympatric Owls," *Condor* 76, no. 1 (Spring 1974): 45–61, https://doi.org/10.2307/1365983.

132 **Eyes weighing in at 32 percent**   Hans Peeters, *Field Guide to Owls of California and the West* (Berkeley: University of California Press, 2007), 17.

132 **Li Bai sees the moonlight . . . Wang Wei plays his *qin***   Wang Wei translation by the author. Li Bai's "Thoughts on a Quiet Night" and Wang Wei's "Bamboo Retreat" are found in the bilingual edition of *Poems of the Masters: China's Classic Anthology of T'ang and Sung Dynasty Verse*, trans. Red Pine (Port Townsend, WA: Copper Canyon Press, 2003), 65, 33.

132 **Han Shan sits outside his hut**   See, for instance, poem 287 in *The Collected Songs of Cold Mountain*, trans. Red Pine (Port Townsend, WA: Copper Canyon Press, 2000), 243.

133 **Peeters shares some examples**   Peeters, *Owls of California*, 23.

CHAPTER 12: LIGHT OF THE OASIS

141 **"They chatter like blackbirds"**   Thoreau was describing Baltimore orioles, but the observation is equally apropos in the case of hooded orioles. Thoreau, *The Journal*, May 8, 1852 in *Thoreau on Birds*, 287.

142 **"Americanized Neotropical beauty"**   Dunne, *Pete Dunne's Essential Field Guide Companion*, 659.

142 **Dawson's chosen epithets**   Dawson, *Birds of California*, 90–91.

144 **We called them palm-leaf orioles**   Florence Merriam Bailey, "The Palm-Leaf Oriole," *Auk* 27, no. 1 (January 1910): 33–35, https://doi.org/10.2307/4070981.

147 **Peattie paints their portrait**   Donald Culross Peattie, *A Natural History of Western Trees* (New York: Bonanza Books, 1950), 296–99.

CHAPTER 13: THE BEAUTIFUL PURIFIER

152 **"But how beautiful he looked"**   Robinson Jeffers, "Vulture," in *The Selected Poetry of Robinson Jeffers* (New York: Random House, 1966).

153 **"[T]he equivalent of perching in the sky"**   Bernd Heinrich, *Life Everlasting* (New York: Houghton Mifflin Harcourt, 2012), 84.

154 **"[C]ontorted soaring"**   Julie M. Mallon, Keith L. Bildstein, and Todd E. Katzner, "In-Flight Turbulence Benefits Soaring Birds," *Auk* 133, no. 1 (January 2016): 79–85, https://doi.org/10.1642/AUK-15-114.1.

157 **The olfactory bulbs of *Cathartes aura***   Nathan P. Grigg, Justin M. Krilow, Cristian Gutierrez-Ibanez, Douglas R. Wylie, Gary R. Graves, and Andrew N. Iwaniuk, "Anatomical Evidence for Scent Guided

Foraging in the Turkey Vulture," *Scientific Reports* 7, no. 17408 (December 2017): 1–10, https://doi.org/10.1038/s41598-017-17794-0.

157 **Twenty-three out of twenty-four of these hidden carcasses** David C. Houston, "Scavenging Efficiency of Turkey Vultures in Tropical Forest," *Condor* 88, no. 3 (August 1986): 318–23, https://doi .org/10.2307/1368878.

158 **The dire consequences** See, for instance, the recent collapse in Indian vulture populations. Meir Rinde, "Poison Pill: The Mysteri- ous Die-Off of India's Vultures," *Science History Institute*, September 3, 2019, https://www.sciencehistory.org/distillations/poison-pill-the -mysterious-die-off-of-indias-vultures.

159 **Montaigne** Michel de Montaigne, "De l'exercitation," in *Les Essais* (1595; repr., Paris: *Le Livre de Poche*, 2001), 592–93.

160 **Ivan Illich** Ivan Illich, *Medical Nemesis: The Expropriation of Health* (New York: Random House, 1976).

160 **"The miseries of the battle-field"** Ralph Waldo Emerson, "Mary Moody Emerson," in *The Complete Works of Ralph Waldo Emerson: Vol. 10, Lectures and Biographical Sketches* (Boston: Houghton Mifflin, 1904), 423.

CHAPTER 14: THE VIEW FROM ABOVE

163 **The View from Above** For the philosophical heritage of the ven- erable practice of envisioning a literal "view from above," practiced enthusiastically by Pythagoreans, Platonists, Stoics, and Epicu- reans alike, see Pierre Hadot, *Qu'est-ce que la philosophie antique?* (Paris: Gallimard, 1995), 316: "To look from above . . . is to regard things with detachment, distance, retrospection, objectivity, such as they are in themselves, placing them within the immensity of the universe, in the totality of nature, without adding to them the false prestige that our passions and human conventions lend them. The view from above changes our judgment of the value of things. Luxury, power, war, frontiers, the worries of daily life become ridic- ulous." (Translation by the author)

167 **Hunting is not the primary objective** Joan M. Ballam, "The Use of Soaring by the Red-Tailed Hawk (*Buteo jamaicensis*)," *Auk* 101, no. 3 (July 1984): 519–24, https://doi.org/10.1093/auk/101.3.519.

172 **"What but fear winged the birds?"** Robinson Jeffers, "The Bloody Sire," in *Selected Poems* (New York: Random House, 1965).

173 **"We all strive for safety"** "Thinking Like a Mountain," in Leopold, *Sand County Almanac*, 133.

CHAPTER 15: A LITTLE MIRACLE

179 **"If I could only do that"** Roland B. Dixon, "Maidu Myths," *Bulletin*

of the American Museum of Natural History 17, no. 2 (June 1902): 90.

179 **Speeds as high as 60 mph**   Christopher James Clark, "Courtship Dives of Anna's Hummingbird Offer Insights into Flight Performance Limits," *Proceedings of the Royal Society B* 276, no. 1670 (September 2009): 3047, https://doi.org/10.1098/rspb.2009.0508.

179 **Their brain center that processes visual information**   Andrea H. Gaede, Benjamin Goller, Jessica P.M. Lam, Douglas R. Wylie, and Douglas L. Altshuler, "Neurons Responsive to Global Visual Motion Have Unique Tuning Properties in Hummingbirds," *Current Biology* 26 (December 2016): 1–7, http://dx.doi.org/10.1016/j.cub.2016.11.041.

180 **They consume calories at seventy-seven times the rate of humans**   Lucy Hicks, "To Survive Frigid Nights, Hummingbirds Cool Themselves to Record-Low Temperatures," *Science*, September 8, 2020, https://doi.org/10.1126/science.abe7185.

180 **An "extreme nap"**   Veronique Greenwood, "These Hummingbirds Take Extreme Naps. Some May Even Hibernate," *New York Times*, September 8, 2020, https://www.nytimes.com/2020/09/08/science/hummingbirds-torpor-hibernation.html.

180 **The pumping of her blood accelerates by a factor of twenty**   Numbers represent an approximate range recorded across several hummingbird species; torpid rates below 50 bpm and active rates above 1,200 bpm were recorded in Robert C. Lasiewski, "Body Temperatures, Heart and Breathing Rate, and Evaporative Water Loss in Hummingbirds," *Physiological Zoology* 37, no. 2 (April 1964): 212–23, https://doi.org/10.1086/physzool.37.2.30152332.

181 **William Bullock**   Quoted in Rachel Poliquin, *The Breathless Zoo: Taxidermy and the Cultures of Longing* (University Park: Pennsylvania State University Press, 2012), 43.

182 **Pablo Neruda**   Translation by the author. Pablo Neruda, "Oda al picaflor," in *Selected Odes of Pablo Neruda* (Berkeley: University of California Press, 2011), 226.

184 **In a time of darkness**   Several variations are recounted in C. Hart Merriam, *The Dawn of the World* (Cleveland: Arthur H. Clark Company, 1910), 89–90.

185 **"[T]he land of flowers and hummingbirds"**   Merriam, *A-Birding on a Bronco*, 147.

185 **René Lesson**   René Primevère Lesson, *Histoire naturelle des oiseaux-mouches* (Paris: Arthus Bertrand, 1829), 205.

186 **Audubon corroborates**   Maria R. Audubon, *Audubon and His Journals* (New York: Charles Scribner's Sons, 1897), 314.

About the Author

Jack Gedney was born in California, moved around the country in his youth, and returned to his home state to complete his education, studying literature and natural history at UC Berkeley. He is also the author of a compact field guide to the trees of the San Francisco Bay Area and coowner of Wild Birds Unlimited in Novato, California.